Anonymous

The Bridgewater Book

Anonymous

The Bridgewater Book

ISBN/EAN: 9783337143343

Printed in Europe, USA, Canada, Australia, Japan

Cover: Foto ©ninafisch / pixelio.de

More available books at **www.hansebooks.com**

The
BRIDGEWATER BOOK

ILLUSTRATED

BOSTON
GEORGE H. ELLIS, PRINTER, 272 CONGRESS STREET
1899

CONTENTS.

		PAGE
BRIDGWATER IN ENGLAND		5
THE SETTLEMENT HERE		7
JAMES KEITH		8
WEST BRIDGEWATER	*Francis E. Howard*	9
THE HOWARD SEMINARY	*Francis E. Howard*	11
EAST BRIDGEWATER	*Hon. Benjamin W. Harris*	12
NORTH BRIDGEWATER AND BROCKTON	*Bradford Kingman*	16
BRIDGEWATER		19
A COMMON WEED	*John White Chadwick*	24
RECOLLECTIONS OF BRIDGEWATER	{ *Lucia Alden Bradford Knapp* *John White Chadwick* }	25
AT SCHOOL: FROM FOUR TO SIXTEEN	*Martha Keith*	27
THE MEMORIAL LIBRARY	*Theodore F. Wright, Ph.D.*	29
THE STATE NORMAL SCHOOL	*Albert G. Boyden*	31
PARISH AND CHURCH IN THE OLD TIMES		33
THE STATE FARM	*Hollis M. Blackstone*	37
MINISTRIES		39
THE OLD BRIDGEWATER HISTORICAL SOCIETY		40

EDITORIAL.

THE views marked in one corner with a K are engraved from photographs taken by Mr. Charles H. King, of Bridgewater, who can supply copies of these and of many others. Most of the views on the second East Bridgewater plate and several on the first plate are from photographs taken by Mr. Joseph C. Crocker, and others (the weir, bridge, pond, and store) by Mr. Charles E. Bennett, both of East Bridgewater. At the foot of the first Bridgewater plate are views of the new and old railroad stations. The latter picture and that of the Oak Street Bridge were taken by Mr. Albert W. Bowman. The view of the Common at the foot of the third Bridgewater plate was taken from the Academy grounds by Mr. George H. Townsend.

In the frontispiece High Street crosses the foreground; and Broad Street, coming from East Bridgewater, descends the hill (with the electric car poles) to the centre of the picture. The Normal School roof and the steeples of the First Parish and Central Square churches are seen against the sky. The Fair Grounds are on the left side of the centre; the shoe-shop, Eagle Cotton-gin works and foundry, on the right. This view was taken by Mr. King.

The flowers and the Iron Works bell tower were drawn by Mrs. T. H. Andrews. The article on Bridgewater was prepared from memoranda supplied by Mr. Joshua E. Crane, and has been revised by him. The article on Parish and Church is based on Edward Buck's "Massachusetts Ecclesiastical Law," (Boston, 1866), which is in the Boston Athenæum Library, Ellis's and Byington's books on the Puritans, and Palfrey's New England.

BRIDGWATER IN ENGLAND.

T is one of the chief towns of pleasant Somersetshire in South-western England, ranking in the county fourth in size, a busy, prosperous, seaport town of fifteen thousand people. It is compactly built, like most English towns; for once they were walled about to make them secure in turbulent times, and the houses had to be crowded together. Through the middle of it flows to the north the river Parret, turbid and tawny with the sand and mud brought up by the strong tides from the Bristol Channel, six miles away in a direct line, but twelve miles off by the winding course of the stream. The sediment of the river, left plentifully on the sloping banks after every tide, has long been used to make what is known in commerce and housekeeping as Bath or Bristol brick. The manufacture of this is an important business here, because only within a short distance of this town, up or down the river, can the mud be found in its best quality. There is only one highway bridge over the river, the railroad bridge crossing a little further down the stream; and this highway bridge, made of iron, is nearly in the centre of the town. Two views of it, looking to the north from the upper stream and from opposite banks, are given in the plate of pictures. The river at low tide is little more than a brook, but at high tide it is about forty-eight feet wide at the bridge. In one of the views the masts of ships are seen in the distance. They cannot come above the bridges; and in a huge dock on the west side of the river below the railroad bridge they find shelter from the dangerous tides, which sometimes rise thirty-six feet and occasionally send up the river a "bore," or perpendicular wave, six or eight feet high. The barges seen in the river above the bridge are used for navigation up the river and its branches as far as Taunton, Ilchester, Glastonbury, and other important towns. Fore Street, of which a view is given, leads from the west end of the bridge to the market (seen here in the distance and pictured in another view) and to St. Mary's, the "parish church" or central house of worship of the "Established Church," or Episcopalian order. High Street is on the north, or right hand, of the market, and is one of the important streets, having the chief hotels and many shops. The private house, in a view by itself, is the residence of the present mayor of the town, Thomas Good, Esq., solicitor. The view is taken from the garden in the rear of the house, and shows the drawing-room windows.

The neighboring country is flat for several miles, especially to the east, where Sedgemoor lies, the scene of the bloody defeat of the Duke of Monmouth's rebel army, July 6, 1685, which was followed by many frightful executions in Bridgwater and all Somersetshire by the victorious army and next September by the infamous Judge Jeffreys, of whom Macaulay has told the story in his History of England. The battle is vividly described in Blackmore's "Lorna Doone." It was "the last fight, deserving the name of a battle," says Macaulay, "that has been fought on English ground." Taunton, a larger town, is about ten miles west of south, on a branch of the Parret, and is connected with Bridgwater by highway, railroad, and canal. North of Taunton stretch to the Bristol Channel, and six or ten miles west of Bridgwater, the high Quantock Hills, from which there are fine views.

The Bridgewater Book

This part of Somerset is romantic with traditions of King Alfred, the brave and wise Saxon chief who finally delivered West England from the invading Danes. It was peculiarly his country. The "isle" of Athelney, about six miles south of Bridgwater, in what was then a marsh, but is now a drained and fertile region, was his refuge from the Danes in 878, when they pressed him hard, just before his final campaign and victory. The Danes were encamped near Bridgwater, having landed from the Bristol Channel. Alfred disguised himself as a harper, and visited the Danish camps. It is at Athelney, according to the old legend, that Alfred, hiding among the peasants, was scolded by a peasant's wife, who did not know him, for letting her cakes burn by the fire, when he had been charged to watch them. This region is also King Arthur's country, the British chief who fought the Saxon invaders, according to a dim tradition, nearly four hundred years before. He was said to be buried in Glastonbury, about twelve miles east of Bridgwater. Still earlier, when the Romans for nearly four centuries ruled in England, there was a prosperous town here; and probably long previously there was a fortified village, which grew up on account of this only ford through the river, to which many roads centred, and also on account of the seaport down the river.

The ford gave the name of Brugie, or bridge, to the village in Saxon times. When William the Conqueror after 1066 parcelled England out among his Norman barons, Brugie and the vicinity were given to a Baron Walter, and the place began to be known as Brugie-Walter, or Walter's Bridge, which finally became Bridgwater. In 1201 Lord William Brewer, who had succeeded to the Walter rights and began to build, in place of the old Saxon wooden bridge, a three-arched stone bridge which stood for more than five hundred years until replaced by an iron bridge, was given permission by King John to build, for the protection of the bridge and close to it, just north of the present Fore Street, a huge castle, surrounded by a moat thirty feet wide, one of the largest and strongest castles in England. Around this castle a town gradually grew up, in place of the primitive small Saxon village, which was generally the way in which towns grew up under the shelter of a baron's castle in those feudal ages. In 1645, when Bridgwater had become the most important town in South-western England, the town and castle were fiercely assaulted by Cromwell's army during the Civil War, and were surrendered with a garrison of 1,600 officers and soldiers. As late as 1810 some of the walls were still standing, but all have now disappeared.

For some years before the Civil War in England there was a large migration of Puritans to New England, who lovingly transplanted many of their cherished customs and even the names of the towns and villages where they had lived, so that their homes in this wilderness across the ocean might as much as possible remind them of their old homes in their mother land. Somersetshire had long been famous for its adventurous mariners and merchants, and the Puritans were numerous in this town and its neighborhood. It is said that our Taunton in Massachusetts was named in compliment to one of its early settlers, Miss Elizabeth Poole, who was born near the English Taunton; and it is probable that our Bridgewater, being settled soon after Taunton, was named on account of the home affection of some of its first inhabitants. Mitchells and Hoopers and Bryants and Allens were prominent citizens in the English town, these names being found in the lists of mayors and members of Parliament; and they are also familiar names in the history of our New England town.

THE SETTLEMENT HERE.

FOR twelve years after the landing of the Pilgrim Fathers in 1620, Plymouth was the only town in the colony. A few small settlements gradually grew up along the coast, so that Duxbury was incorporated in 1632 and Scituate in 1636. Far to the west, by the tide-waters of Narragansett Bay, Taunton was settled by families from Massachusetts Bay in 1637 and incorporated in 1639. But the higher land between Plymouth and Taunton, mostly drained by the branches of a stream which flows into Narragansett Bay, and separated from the Plymouth slopes by the Pembroke and Halifax hills, remained the forest home of Indians, whose chief was Massasoit, later known as Ousamequin, the hospitable savage who had befriended the first settlers on the coast. In 1645, however, Miles Standish and other Duxbury men received permission from the Old Colony government to buy of the Indians in this wilderness sixty-four square miles, afterward increased to about eighty-six,—of which the centre was at a spot now marked by a stone near the Westdale station,—as compensation for the loss of territory from Duxbury when Marshfield was taken from this town. In 1649 a deed of this land was signed by Ousamequin on Sachem's rock, as tradition says, near the present Carver Cotton-gin Works; and the land was first called "Duxbury New Plantation."

There was also a migration from Massachusetts Bay, Deacon Samuel Edson coming from Salem about 1650, and settling in what is now West Bridgewater on the south side of the river, now called the Town River, just above where the Howard, or Tavern, Bridge now stands. And, because this was the richest land in the whole region, some of the Duxbury people who had taken shares in the purchase settled near him about the same time on scattered farms along the river from below the present village of West Bridgewater gradually extending up the river to within a mile of the head of it in Lake Nippenicket. One of the first of these was John Howard, whose house was the first tavern, for more than a century the only tavern, in the region; and for a long time the bridge near by was the only bridge over the river. This was therefore the centre to which all the primitive paths converged,—one from the Massachusetts Bay towns on the north, known as "the Bay path"; two others to the south-east, along the river on opposite sides of it, through the wilderness which is now Bridgewater, on the way to Plymouth; and others through the woods north and south of Lake Nippenicket to Taunton on the south-west, where the first settlers went to trade and carried grist on foot.

In 1656 the town was incorporated as Bridgewater, being the first town settled away from the coast within the Old Colony limits. It was the northern part of the valley of the Taunton River, which is the junction (near Paper-mill Village, or Pratt-town, in Bridgewater) of the Town River, flowing from West Bridgewater, and the Satucket, of which the Matfield is a branch, both flowing from East Bridgewater. The Taunton River separates Bridgewater from Middleboro, and runs off to the westward to Taunton, and then southward. This town at first included what is now Brockton and the greater part of the original town of Abington (set off in 1712, and embracing what are now Abington, Rockland, and Whitman) and a part of Hanson.

JAMES KEITH.

THE first minister of Bridgewater was born about 1643, in Scotland across the ocean, was educated in Aberdeen University, and came to Boston about 1662, when probably eighteen years old. He was introduced to the Bridgewater church by Dr. Increase Mather, of Boston, who wrote of him in later years as "that gracious, faithful, humble servant of God," and referred to "his painful"—that is, painstaking or conscientious,—"and patient conduct." He seems to have preached here as merely a "student in divinity." Tradition says he preached his first sermon on "pulpit rock," near the river in the mill meadow just behind the present post-office, from Jer. i. 6,—"Behold, I cannot speak; for I am a child." In 1664 the town voted to settle him, and give him "a purchase right,"—that is, a fifty-sixth part of the original grant, equal to what each of the first settlers had,—"and other lands with a house built thereon," probably the house which the town in 1661 had voted to build. It is said to be the house now owned by George M. Pratt above Howard Bridge on the north side of the river (see the plate); but the east half of the house, on the right hand of the front door as one enters, was added in 1678, and the rear afterward changed. The picture below shows the first form of the house and the usual form of houses then. The town-miller, Deacon Edson, lived just across the river; and the young minister soon wooed and wedded the miller's daughter Susanna. In 1673 the town voted that "Mr. Keith, having been some competent time with them, should have the house and lands where he lived, twelve acres, and a whole purchase right," as had been promised in 1664. His salary was £40 (about $200), half to be paid at Boston in money and the other half at home in produce. In 1667 he was voted an additional grant of thirty cords of wood yearly. In 1681 the salary was raised to £50, and £30 of this to be paid in produce. In 1689 he was allowed £10 in corn instead of the thirty cords of wood.

In 1676 he interceded with the colonial authorities to spare the lives of King Philip's wife and boy, just after the Indian War, and was successful. In 1707 he married a second wife, Mrs. Mary Williams, of Taunton. In 1717, June 4, when seventy-four years old, he preached the sermon at the dedication of the meeting-house in the newly formed South Parish, and in this sermon made a severe reference to the prevalence of drunkenness, "the scandalous and horrible abuse of rum, which threatens ruin unto this land and to this place; a ruin to all our dearest interests, both civil and religious." He died July 23, 1719, aged seventy-six, after fifty-three years' ministry; and his grave is marked by a tomb in the cemetery on South Street near the Tavern Bridge. He left six sons and three daughters, from whom a numerous posterity, scattered in many States, are descended.

WEST BRIDGEWATER.

HE first settlers in the original town of Bridgewater organized the First Church about 1651. Samuel Edson and John Willis are early mentioned as deacons. In 1656 the town was incorporated, and the first town-meeting held November 3. It was "a most praying and most pious town," as the Mathers said; and yet intemperate habits, which were prevalent in New England till after the Revolution, seem to have grown up at even this early time, as is shown by Mr. Keith's remarks in 1717. Soon after 1662 Mr. Keith began his ministry. The poverty of the people made the financial problem as perplexing then, notwithstanding the religiousness of the town, as it has generally been in our New England parishes to the present day; and in 1689 the town instructed "David Perkins, John Ames, and Samuel Washburn to get in Mr. Keith's salary by all loving persuasions and legal means."

In 1661 the first meeting-house was built of logs. A stone shaft on Howard Street, in front of the house of Francis E. Howard, marks the site. The first burying-ground was near by; but the gravestones, as was usual then, were without inscriptions, and in 1853 they were removed by the owner of the land. In 1674 the second meeting-house, forty feet by twenty-six, and fourteen feet high inside, was built where the Soldiers' Monument now stands at the present "centre," and a new burying-ground was opened some distance to the north of the meeting-house.

The first tavern, which for more than a century was probably the only tavern in West and South Bridgewater, stood at the corner of Howard and River Streets, near what was long known as Tavern Bridge. The present bridge here was built about 1832, and is often known as Howard Bridge. (See the plate.) As early as 1670 John Howard was licensed to keep the tavern; his son, John, Jr., followed; John, Jr.'s son, Major Edward; the major's son, Colonel Edward; and, after him, the colonel's widow, Mrs. Abigail till 1812. Thus it was kept by the same family for one hundred and fifty years.

In 1716, the south part of the town being set off, the rest was known as the North Parish till 1723, when it was divided into the West and East Parishes. In 1738 portions of these were set off as the North Parish.

Mr. Keith died in 1719; and in 1721 Daniel Perkins was ordained, ministering for sixty-one years, till his death in 1782. He probably lived in a house that stood where E. Bradford Wilbur's stands now, on Centre Street, the second from the Soldiers' Monument toward Westdale. It was said that his ministry was "not only long, but peaceful and efficacious," from which it might be inferred, as none of his sermons are printed, that he was more successful as a pastor than as a preacher. In 1731 the third meeting-house was built on the site of the second. It was long known as the Old Town-house, or the "Three Decker," on account of the three rows of windows. After 1801 this was used for town purposes only, as the Parish built a new house for religious services; and it was taken down in 1823, after the other parishes became towns. For nearly one hundred and fifty years the people of all the Bridgewaters came to this spot for their town-meetings.

The Bridgewater Book

At the time of King Philip's war, 1675, there were only sixty-four men who were over nineteen years of age in the primitive settlement. Nearly a century later, in 1764, there were 106 houses and 121 families in this Parish, and the population was 880. In 1810 it was 1,065. It diminished during the next twenty years, when there were large migrations; but in 1840 it began to grow.

In 1780 John Reed, a son of the Rev. Solomon Reed of Titicut, and afterward a Doctor of Divinity, was ordained as colleague of Mr. Perkins, and, after fifty-one years' ministry, died in 1831, seventy-nine years old. During his time a Baptist society was formed in 1785, which died out before 1833, and was revived in 1835. The Cocheset Methodist society was formed in 1832. In 1801 the Parish built the fourth meeting-house, which is now the Unitarian church, remodelled in 1847. Dr. Reed was called an able and sound divine, and was very much valued in ecclesiastical councils. He was in Congress from 1795 to 1801, and was a friend of Washington, who sometimes invited him to dinner and seated him on his right hand. Many years before his death he became blind; but he continued to preach, and, with his psalm book open in his hand, he would recite a whole versified Psalm from memory, and also the Scripture lesson. He lived next to Rev. Mr. Perkins's house, in a house on Centre Street, which is the third on the left hand from the Soldiers' Monument on the way to Westdale.

William Baylies was the only other Congressman resident in this Parish. He was four years in Congress. He came here in 1799, was never married, and died in 1865. He lived for more than sixty years in the Judge Howard house on South Street (see the plate) which was built in 1797 by Judge Daniel Howard, who died in 1833. It was said at the time to be the finest house in the Bridgewaters. He was at the head of the bar in Plymouth, Bristol, and Norfolk Counties; and his influence over a jury was said to be greater than that of any other lawyer of his day. William Cullen Bryant, whose grandfather, Dr. Philip Bryant (died 1816), was a physician in the North Parish, and whose father, Dr. Peter, moved to Cummington, came back to his ancestral town, and studied law with Mr. Baylies for more than a year.

Another family of which the descendants have been prominent is the Ames family. Oliver, who was a manufacturer of shovels, born in 1777, moved to Easton, where his sons and grandsons built up the great shovel factory, and have been eminent in public life.

In 1822 this West Parish became a town. In 1834 Richard Stone was ordained here as minister, and served till 1842; but in 1836 the society and town were separated here as elsewhere in the State, and this First Parish Society was known as the First Congregational, or Unitarian, Society.

In 1840 the village of Cocheset began to grow up, and the first Methodist church was built there, the second in 1844. In 1879 the Soldiers' Monument (see view of "the centre") was dedicated, and in 1889 the present Baptist church. In 1893 part of the northern end of the town was ceded to Brockton. In 1894 the Grange Building was erected.

In 1840 the population was 1,201; in 1870, 1,803; in 1890, 1,917. It remains to-day, as it has always been, a quiet agricultural town, one of the best farming towns in the county, with healthy air and beautiful scenery.

FRANCIS E. HOWARD.

THE HOWARD SEMINARY.

ENJAMIN BEAL HOWARD, a native of West Bridgewater and a resident for upward of sixty years, died in New Bedford, April 3, 1867. Soon after his death it was ascertained that by his will he had left $80,000 for the establishing of a High School or Seminary of Learning in West Bridgewater. He left this money in the care of eleven persons, to expend the income, but no part of the principal, in support of the school. The persons appointed trustees were the following : Azel Howard, Benjamin Howard, and Francis E. Howard (his three sons), John E. Howard, Otis Drury, Austin Packard, Pardon Copeland, James Copeland, George D. Ryder, Jonathan C. Keith, and John M. Lothrop, all of whom are now deceased except Francis E. Howard, of West Bridgewater, and John E. Howard, of Brockton, the latter of whom is not a trustee now, having resigned December 25, 1875.

The present board of trustees consists of Francis E. Howard, president; Isaac N. Nutter, of East Bridgewater, vice-president; Benjamin B. Howard, secretary and treasurer; Andrew J. Bailey, of Boston; the Rev. Edward B. Maglathlin, of North Easton; Wallace C. Keith, of Brockton; Bradford Copeland, Clinton P. Howard, Charles R. Packard, and Charles E. Tisdale, of West Bridgewater; and there is one vacancy. In April, 1868, the trustees purchased of the late Mr. Jonathan Howard ten acres of land for $2,500 on which to erect the school buildings. In May, 1875, the work of building was begun, and in the following year completed. In this year, 1876, the late Otis Drury provided the trustees with the bell now on the Seminary. At his death he willed his whole property, after the death of his widow, amounting to nearly $70,000, to the Seminary, of which the interest only should be expended.

In the fall of 1875 the subject of a Girls' School was first agitated. In May, 1883, through the influence of the Rev. Dr. Edward Everett Hale, the trustees engaged Miss Helen Magill, daughter of Edward H. Magill, President of Swarthmore College, Pennsylvania, to open a Girls' School, which was called The Howard Collegiate Institute, and to continue in charge for five years. During this year, 1883, a Boarding Hall, forty by eighty feet, was built, which accommodated thirty pupils. This is seen in the pictures, on one side of the Seminary Hall, and is known as Drury Hall. The school increased in numbers and reputation to such a degree that in the summer of 1885 it was necessary to enlarge this hall, so as to accommodate sixteen more pupils. In 1887, after four years' service, Miss Magill resigned. The trustees engaged Miss Emma O. Conro, for a year previous assistant to Miss Magill. She remained principal for three years. In September, 1890, Mr. Horace M. Willard, formerly principal of Bridgewater Academy, was engaged for one year; and at his suggestion the name of the school was changed to Howard Seminary. He was then engaged for five years from July 1, 1891; and after six years of great success he resigned, and was succeeded by Mr. Ralph W. Gifford, who after two years resigned to engage in another profession. He was succeeded by the present principal, Miss Sarah E. Laughton, in September, 1898, whose administration for the past year has been such as to assure a larger attendance, a more extensive reputation, and a more successful school.

FRANCIS E. HOWARD.

EAST BRIDGEWATER.

N 1722 the inhabitants of the east end of the North Precinct of Bridgewater petitioned the legislature to be set off as a separate precinct, stating "that they now look upon themselves as capable of giving an honorable support to a minister"; and on December 14, 1723, the East Precinct was incorporated.

The settlement began early. Samuel Allen, Jr., the first settler, is said to have been here by 1660. He built his house on the east side of the Matfield, near where the Bridgewater Branch Railroad crosses it to-day, on land of the late John Lane. Nicholas Byram, and his son-in-law, Thomas Whitman, came here in 1662; Robert Latham, in 1663; and by 1673, when their father, Arthur Harris, made his will, Isaac and Samuel Harris owned lands on both sides of Satucket River, and each had a house on the north side.

Samuel Allen, Jr., owned land extending north from Matfield River, including the eastern part of the present village, the old cemetery, and the Common. Nicholas Byram owned five of the fifty-four shares of the original proprietors, including the west part of the village and a large tract west of Snell Meadow brook. He built his house just west of the brook, on or near the spot where the late Jotham Hicks built the house now standing. Thomas Whitman owned the peninsula lying between the Satucket and Matfield Rivers, including all the lands now owned by the sons of the late Zebina Keith and the Carver Cotton-gin Company. The house of Deacon John Whitman, who died there at the age of a hundred and seven years, stands on the north side of Whitman Street, on land owned by his ancestor Thomas. Robert Latham came from Marshfield, and became the owner of a very large tract on the south side of Satucket River, including a large part of what is now commonly called Satucket. It included Sachem's Rock and Standish Grove, the latter of which is now the property of the Bridgewater Historical Society. Arthur Harris and his two sons owned land adjoining Latham, on the north. Isaac Harris married Latham's daughter. The Deacon Azor Harris house, now owned by his son Arthur, stands on Latham land; it is a hundred and fifty-five years old, the oldest in the village, having been built in 1745 by Robert Latham, son of Chilton Latham, who was the son of the first Robert, and lived in this house with his son Robert six years after it was built, and died in 1751, aged eighty.

From 1660 to 1700 the population increased rapidly. Joseph Shaw, the ancestor of the Bridgewater family, settled by 1699 at what is now known as Shaw's Mills. His descendants are numerous and distinguished. The late Chief Justice Lemuel Shaw is of the third generation, through the Rev. John, of the South Parish, and his son, the Rev. Oakes, of Barnstable. Isaac Alden, a grandson of John, the Pilgrim, settled here about 1685, and owned a large tract on Beaver Brook, building a house near what is now Jones's Mill, in the north part of the present town. He was a brother of Joseph, who settled in what is now Bridgewater, on the south side of Sprague's Hill. Elmwood was settled by Elisha Hayward and Nathaniel Hayward, Jr., Jonathan Hill, Edward son of Experience Mitchell, who came in the "Ann" in 1622, and John Howard.

During King Philip's war, in 1676, this part of the old town suffered severely. All the houses except that of Nicholas Byram were burned by the Indians.

OLD FORGE SITE

CENTRAL ST

OLD BRICK STORE

INDIAN HERRING WEIR

ELM-WOOD

CHAMBERLAIN BRIDGE

ELMWOOD

MILL-POND
SATUCKET

Robert Latham built a saw-mill on Satucket River, just below the Indian herring-weir, and behind the old Benjamin Harris house, now owned by the heirs of Warren Bennett. The dam of this mill overflowed the old weir, so that it ceased to be visible except in times of repair, when the water was drawn off. This mill became the property of Isaac Harris, and remained there till 1726, when Isaac Harris, Thomas Whitman, and Jonathan Bass, as partners, built a new mill at what is now the Carver Cotton-gin Company's dam. But the new dam raised a pond, which also covered the old weir, so that for many years it has not been seen until this summer (1899), when the pond has been drawn down for extensive repairs. The weir, as shown in one of the plates, consists of two low walls of stone, extending down stream from each bank to near the centre of the stream, but not quite meeting. The fish in going up to their spawning grounds above, in the spring, were obliged to pass through this narrow opening, where they could be caught by nets or spears in great quantities. Within even the last hundred years this river supplied an abundance of alewives, or herrings. Not until the mills below began to maintain their dams at all seasons of the year, did this valuable fishery perish. It may be that at no distant day, when steam or electric power shall have taken the place of water power, these waters may be again stocked with fish, to the great benefit of the people. If such should be the result, any one who will study the map of Plymouth County, and see the vast pond and water area, once the spawning ground of the alewives, may be able to get some idea of the immense supply of fish food that could be provided for the people.

Many of the Indians continued to live here. Some of them served in the Revolutionary army, and the last was living here as late as 1843.

In 1721 a meeting-house had been begun on land given by Samuel Allen, Jr., apparently in anticipation of the legal organization of the precinct in 1723. On April 14, 1724, John Angier was called "to settle with them in the work of the ministry according to the gospel," and was ordained October 28, 1724, over a church of thirty-three members, twelve men and twenty-one women, which was organized at the same time. He was then twenty-three years old. November 23, 1732, he married Mary Bourne, of Sandwich. His house, now removed, stood on the site of Mrs. Millet's house, on the side of the Common opposite the Unitarian church. His pastorate continued till his death, April 14, 1787, or more than sixty-two years. The meeting-house was finished in time for the ordination. It was probably forty feet square, with sixteen-feet posts. There were eleven "pues" on the floor next the walls, an open space in the centre for long benches, and nine pews in the gallery. The Indians were allowed to make pews for themselves under the stairs.

During this ministry the parish grew in population, and became one of the most important manufacturing centres in the State. There have been no less than twenty-two mill sites in the town, many of them now disused. The first mill was Robert Latham's, already mentioned, possibly built as early as 1667, and removed in 1726. Shaw's Mills, so called, were built before 1700, probably consisting of grist-mill and saw-mill, and were of great use till destroyed by fire some years ago. The old forge, built in 1726 by Captain Jonathan Bass, over the Salisbury River, was in constant use in converting scrap iron into bars and shapes down to 1884 or 1885, when new methods prevailed. About 1740 Hugh Orr, who was born in Scotland in 1717, erected mills on Matfield River, at the south side of the present stone bridge, and in 1742 the house now standing at Vinton's corner, so called, owned by William Vinton, his descendant. In these mills he ground grain, made scythes, axes, and other edged tools, muskets, bored cannon for the use of the State during the Revolution, and made machinery for carding and spinning and weaving cotton and cleaning flaxseed. He was the first man in America to cast cannon solid and then bore them out, and his trip-hammer shop was the first of the kind in this part of the land. He was an active, skilled, and inventive mechanic, and rendered very valuable service to his community during his long life of sixty years in this his adopted country. He died December 6, 1798, aged eighty-one.

The water power at Satucket, now owned by the Carver Company, has, since the first building of the dam in 1726, been in constant service until the present time; and to-day a larger, more varied, and probably more profitable business is being carried on than ever before. On that dam, from an early date down to 1872, when the mills were burned, nails and tacks were largely manufactured by David Kingman and Zebina Keith and his sons.

The shoe manufacturing business, which is now such an enormous business in Brockton and neighboring towns in this county, may be said to have originated in this town. In Elmwood Village, on the Mitchell farm, just south of the bridge on the west side of the road, the son, grandson, and great-grandsons carried on the business of tanning and currying leather. The writer of this article well remembers the time when tanning was done there. And it dates back to 1700.

In 1822 Cushing Mitchell and Seth Bryant, the former a grandson and the latter a great-grandson of Colonel Edward Mitchell, who succeeded Ensign Edward Mitchell, his father, in the tannery business in Elmwood, formed a partnership under the name of Mitchell & Bryant, and commenced the manufacture there of "sale shouse," as they were called in distinction from custom shoes. They conducted a large business, for the time, down to the panic of 1837, when they met with financial disaster. Mr. Bryant afterward conducted the business there, and during the Civil War made sewed shoes for the army successfully and in large quantities.

In 1754 the second meeting-house was completed. It was fifty-six feet by forty-five, and twenty-two feet high. It was built east of the old house, which was allowed to stand till the new house was ready. Hugh Orr purchased the old house and used the lumber to build his mill on the Matfield River, in which he bored and finished cannon during the Revolution. In 1764 there were 142 houses, 157 families, and 959 population.

In 1767, December 23, Samuel Angier, son of the Rev. John, was ordained colleague pastor; and after his father's death in 1787 he continued in service till his death, Jan. 18, 1805, at the age of sixty-one, after thirty-eight years' ministry.

During his ministry the third or present meeting-house was built, in 1795, on the site of the first house, sixty-eight feet by fifty-four, and twenty-eight feet high. It stood broadside to the street, with a spire at the west end and a porch at the east end, both containing stairways to the galleries; and with three entrances, one in the middle of the long front, which opened on a broad aisle, and the others at the two ends opening on the cross aisle. The pulpit with its sounding-board and the deacons' seats in front of the pulpit were in the centre of the north, or rear, side of the house. In 1850 the house was turned one-quarter round, so that the steeple is at the front, with a somewhat enlarged porch. The other porch was removed, the pulpit placed where this porch once stood, all the old pews removed and the present pews put in. The second house stood till the third was occupied; and it was then sold to General Sylvanus Lazell, who some years afterward used the old material in the erection of his mansion in 1799, now the picturesque home of Mr. Henry Hobart. And it is supposed that some of the lumber

CATHOLIC  METHODIST  UNION

was used about 1820 in building a house for his grandson, Sylvanus Lazell Mitchell, pictured as the "Judge Harris House" in the plate. But this house has been much changed and enlarged.

In 1806 James Flint was ordained the fourth minister of the parish, and in 1821 was called to Salem. Benjamin Fessenden immediately succeeded him, resigning in 1825. John A. Williams was minister from 1826 to 1828, and Eliphalet P. Crafts from 1828 to 1836, when parishes and towns were finally separated throughout the State, and all religious societies put on an equal footing. In 1824 the congregation that still worshipped in the old meeting-house was authorized by the legislature to be called "The First Parish in East Bridgewater." In 1826 the Union Trinitarian Society was formed, which is now known as the Union Church and Society; in 1831, the New Jerusalem; in 1850, the first Methodist; and in 1862 the Catholic congregation was gathered.

But in 1823, June 14, the parish was incorporated as a town, having then a population of about 1,500; and the seclusion of such a country town seventy-six years ago may be judged from the fact that mails and stages went to Boston three times only in a week.

From 1827 to about 1843 the water power at Satucket was used for the weaving of cotton cloth. Since 1843 the present owners have manufactured cotton-gins on a large scale. Since the fire of 1872, which destroyed nearly all the old structures, new mills have been built and new industries have been introduced. Linter-gins, used in removing the lint from cotton-seed to prepare it for the machinery used in extracting oil from the seed, are largely manufactured by this company under their own exclusive patents. They also manufacture shoe machinery of many kinds and many articles requiring fine mechanical skill. It is now the most important manufacturing company in town, and furnishes constant employment to a large force of first-class workmen.

For many years dating back before the Revolution a slitting and rolling-mill situated below Orr's Works on Matfield River, was carried on by David & George Keith, and by Levi Keith & Sons. In 1835 new mills were erected, and the business greatly enlarged. The mills passed from the old firm into the hands of Rogers & Sheldon, who manufactured nails and rolled bar iron into plates. This firm did a large and profitable business until their mills were burned. This was soon after the great change took place in iron manufactures in this country, when the newly discovered processes of rapidly and cheaply converting pig iron into homogeneous iron, or mild steel, as it was called, were taking the place of the old processes in use by the firm up to that time. This fine water privilege is now idle. May it not, at some future day, be utilized in the production of electric power, light, and heat for the people?

The population has risen from about 1,500 in 1823 to 2,894 in State census of 1895, having lost, by the annexation of portions of its territory to Whitman and Brockton in 1875, about 300 of its population.

In 1874 the Soldiers' Monument was dedicated, and in 1897 the Washburn Library.

The two towns of Bridgewater and East Bridgewater are abundantly supplied with water of great purity from springs and from wells drilled into the granite rock from one hundred to two hundred feet deep, on the south side of Sprague's Hill in Bridgewater.

BENJAMIN W. HARRIS.

NORTH BRIDGEWATER AND BROCKTON.

HE last settled portion of the original town of Bridgewater was the north part, where there was no permanent settlement till after 1700. The interests of the settlers were all concentrated at the old centre, where they resorted for worship and also for such other privileges as were common to the whole population. During 1737 they built a meeting-house in the hopes that a larger number could enjoy religious privileges by having a house nearer home, and, accordingly, Robert Howard and fifty-four others petitioned the legislature to incorporate them into a separate town; but they were granted only an incorporation as a parish, by the name of the North Parish of Bridgewater, Janurary 3, 1738. The first parish meeting was held February 5, 1739; and in December John Porter, of Abington, was asked to preach as a candidate. In 1740, a church was organized, under the name of the Fourth Church in Bridgewater; and on October 15 Mr. Porter was ordained. His qualifications, both natural and acquired, were remarkable. Much that was estimable in his Christian character he gratefully ascribed, under God, to the labors of that justly celebrated and useful servant of Christ, the Rev. Mr. Whitefield, under whose ministry of the word he received the most deep and salutary impressions a little before his ordination. He had formed an intimate acquaintance with Mr. Whitefield, invited him to his pulpit, and enjoyed the benefit of his instruction. He wielded the sword of the spirit with great skill, vigor and success, though never fond of controversy. He was distinguished for his prudence and fidelity, exemplary life and holy conversation. He continued to preach for sixty years, when in 1800, feeling the infirmities of age, he called for a colleague. He died March 12, 1802, eighty-seven years old. To the influence of this good man more than any other thing, is the community indebted for the love of order, industry, economy, enterprise, and religious character of many of the descendants of that society. His influence had much to do with the formation of the character of the early inhabitants of this parish.

The first meeting-house was a small, plain structure, in keeping with the times, facing south, without steeple, bell or chimney. It was on the site of the present stone church of the First Congregational Society. The windows had diamond-shaped glass. The walls were plastered, but there was no stove; for, till the present century, the meeting-houses were never warmed, except as small foot-stoves were often used by the women. The usual practice in building churches then was to finish the inside and sell "pew room," or sections of the floor, which each purchaser would finish to suit himself. These pews were usually six to eight feet front and five or five and a half feet deep. The unmarried men and women were generally put into separate pews in the centre, and there was a partition between the men's and the women's front gallery.

In 1763 the second meeting-house was built of the same size as the house of the South Parish, and the belfry was twelve feet square and eighty-five feet high. A bell was bought in 1764. In 1772 a choir was formed for the first time, and the south part of the women's gallery was assigned to them; in 1775 the north part was assigned; and in 1801 "surkerler" seats were built in front of the gallery for the choir. The negroes were seated in a loft provided for the purpose; but in 1800 there was much feeling because "the blacks" intruded into the white folks' pews. They were then shifted about into different galleries. Efforts were made in 1818-19 to induce the parish to put a stove into the house, as other parishes were doing; but the opposition was too strong. In 1822 the south part of the east gallery was voted "for the use of the young women," who seemed to have been put by themselves. In 1827 the house was taken down.

In 1764 the population was only 833, less than any of the other parishes. There were 131 families and 120 houses.

In 1800, October 15, Asa Meech, the second minister of this parish, was ordained as colleague with Mr. Porter, and preached till 1811, when he resigned. In 1812, October 18, Daniel Huntington was ordained; but on account of ill health he resigned in 1833, and lived in New London, Conn., till 1840, when he was called to the South Church in Campello. Mr. Huntington was of generous sympathies, extremely modest, of pleasing aspect in voice and manner, of genial humor and good judgment, affable, courteous and true, a clear, logical and earnest preacher. He was greatly beloved by all his household, and was distinguished above most others in his consolation to the afflicted and bereaved. In all the churches where he was called for advice he had the confidence and respect of all. He died at New London, Conn., May 21, 1858.

In 1816 the first post-office in this part of Bridgewater was opened. In 1818 the wife of the Rev. Mr. Huntington gathered the first Sunday-school. About 1820 the first public stage ran through the place. In 1821 this parish was incorporated as the town of North Bridgewater. In 1827 the parish built its third meeting-house. The "three easterly pews in the north gallery" were "reserved for young women," and the "south-west and north-west pews" "for the people of colour." In the same year the New Jerusalem Society was organized, and in 1831 the first Methodist. In 1833, September 18, William Thompson was ordained minister of the parish society, and was dismissed in 1834 to fill a professorship. In 1835, October 1, Paul Couch was installed as his successor, and preached here for twenty-four years, till 1859. He possessed the highest type of mental culture, was sincere, earnest and fearless, of ready sympathy for the afflicted, so that his presence was a benediction to every home. As a preacher, he was forcible in manner, and of great freedom and candor. In the year of his installation it was voted to put stoves into the meeting-house for the first time. But in 1836 this society ceased to be the parish society of North Bridgewater, when State and Church were finally separated in Massachusetts; and it took its place as only the First Congregational Society. In the same year the South Congregational Society was formed in what is now Campello and a church was built, which was replaced in 1854 by the present church; and in 1842 the Central Methodist Society was formed.

In 1845 the railroad to Boston was opened, which greatly increased the business facilities of the town. In 1850 the Porter Evangelical and First Baptist Societies were formed, and built houses of worship; and the southern part of the town, which had long been known as "Plain Village," had a post-office established, and began to be known as Campello, a name which means "a little plain," and was suggested by the Rev. Mr. Huntington, then pastor of the South Congregational Church. In 1853 a destructive fire visited Campello, which materially checked the growth of the place. In 1854 the First Congregational Society built their fourth house of worship, which was burned in 1894; and the present stone church was built in 1898. In 1856 the Catholic congregation was organized with a settled pastor, and built a church in 1859. In 1857 the Universalist Society was organized, and in 1863 built its church. In 1859 gas-light was introduced into the town. In 1871 the first Episcopal services were held, and St. Paul's Church was organized. In the same year the Board of Trade was formed, "in order to promote the efficiency and extend the usefulness of the business men of North Bridgewater."

In 1874 the town took the name of Brockton, and within the next ten years the population nearly doubled. In 1881 it was incorporated as a city. In 1810 the population was 1,354; in 1820 it was 1,480, second to the South Parish only among the Bridgewaters; in 1830 it was 1,953, larger than the other Bridgewaters; in 1860 it was 6,384; in 1880 it was 13,608, with 2,662 houses and 2,999 families. It is now about 33,000.

The question is often asked, Why has this city gone forward with such rapid strides? The reply would lead us back to the early settlement of the North Parish. A writer observed many years since that among the influences to which the descendants of the early inhabitants were indebted for the love of order, industry, economy, enterprise and religious character of her people, might be mentioned the unanimity between pastor and people, and a working together for the common good.

In some portions of the old parish there was found iron ore, the making of which into various kinds of implements gave employment to a large number of people. James and Luke Perkins made muskets, small anchors, scythes, shovels, plough points, etc., at the trip-hammer or "water shop," near Salisbury Heights, well known as Sprague's or Factory Village. In 1813 a mill was erected for manufacturing cotton and woollen goods. Hollow ware was made at Howard Mill, on what is now Belmont Street. The works were afterward used for the manufacture of shoe tools. Sidney Perkins made hay forks and manure forks; and the Easton Brothers made spikes, adzes, plane-irons, etc., near Pleasant Street. About 1790 carding and fulling mills were built on Salisbury River, where since that time all kinds of ship-work were made. Of late years the works at this place have been enlarged; and the manufacturing of small nails, tacks, shoe-nails, etc., are carried on largely. Much has also been done in early times in the tannery business. The first grist-mill in this town is now known as the Packard Mill, which was for a long time in charge of the "Honest Miller," Deacon Zenas Packard. The rivers of the town furnish power for many kinds of business. This place long held the reputation of making the best kind of shoe tools, hammers, knives, spoke-shaves, pegging and sewing needles, shoe-pegs, lasts, etc. It has always taken the lead in supplying every kind of goods to the surrounding towns. The first to give push to that line of trade were William F. Brett, in 1834, William H. White, and in 1844 the Hon. Henry W. Robinson, who was for over fifty years in business. A large furniture manufacturing business was conducted by Josiah W. Kingman at Campello from 1825 to 1853, when the establishment was burnt, and for a long time from 1829, at the centre, by Messrs. Howard & Clark.

But the principal industry of Brockton is the manufacture of shoes, and a large number of manufacturers have acquired wealth in this business.

A yearly Agricultural Fair is held here, said to be the most flourishing in the State, if not in New England.

The reader is referred to Kingman's History of North Bridgewater (1866) and History of Brockton (1884) for further details.

BRADFORD KINGMAN.

BRIDGEWATER.

HE Duxbury people, who settled about 1650 in what is now West Bridgewater, took up more land about 1665 further down the river to the south; and pretty early the Leonard, Washburn, and Edson farms included the land now covered by the village of Bridgewater. The first of these, owned by the sons of Solomon Leonard, was where Main Street now runs; the second, owned by John Washburn and his sons, lay below the line where South Street now runs; and the Edson farm was where Pleasant Street now runs, extending nearly to Scotland.

On account of the Indians few other families came. But King Philip's War ended in 1676, and the security that followed drew many new families. The neighborhood called Scotland was early settled by the Fobeses and Keiths, who were Scotch,— this fact probably suggesting the name of the place,— and by the Bassetts and Leaches. Soon after the war, Josiah Edson, a son of Deacon Samuel, built a large house on the way to Scotland. He was known as "old Justice Edson," and was the most important man in this part of the town, owning much land and doing much business. His son, Captain Josiah, was also an important man; and a grandson, Colonel Josiah, controlled the trade of this neighborhood, owning the store at the corner of Main Street, which had previously been established by others. By 1700 the population had much increased, and the main roads of the present Bridgewater had been laid out. In 1692 the whole town, with the rest of the Old Colony, was joined to Massachusetts, from which many settlers had already come.

For nearly a hundred and sixty years, till 1822, the people went to town-meetings in what is now West Bridgewater, the old centre of the town; and for fifty years they attended Sunday services at the same place, till 1716, when this southern part of the town was organized as the South Parish for church and school purposes, and a meeting-house was built near the site of the present First Parish, or Unitarian, church, the Rev. James Keith preaching the dedication sermon, August 14, 1717. The house was forty-three feet by thirty-eight, without tower or belfry. A low partition up the centre separated the men and women, who sat on very rude benches; and the deacons sat in front of the pulpit, facing the people. August 18, the First Church in this parish, of more than fifty members, was organized. Benjamin Allen was immediately engaged to preach, and on July 9, 1718, was formally settled. He probably lived in the Edson-Lazell house, now occupied by Miss Clara Washburn, or certainly very near this site. After thirteen years he was released by a council in 1730, and was afterward settled in Maine, dying there in 1764.

In 1731 began the long and honored ministry of John Shaw, a Bridgewater boy, born in the East Parish, and dying in 1791, at the age of eighty-two, after sixty years' service. His influence was soon felt in various innovations, such as the introduction of many new psalm tunes in 1732. There was no choir till about 1788; and the hymns were read by a deacon in front of the pulpit, each line being read and then sung before the next line was sung, a custom which lasted till 1760. In 1741 the meeting-house was enlarged. In 1760 a new house was built, sixty-four feet by fifty, in the usual shape and style of such buildings then. It was of nearly the size of the present Unitarian church, which is seventy feet long, but the length of it was at right angles to the length of the present church. The main entrance was through the porch on the east side, where the spire now is, and the pulpit was on the west side. The tower was on the north end, where there was another entrance. (See the cut below.) It was enlarged in 1810, and was used for eighty-five years, till 1845. The first meeting-house was like it, but had no tower and was smaller. In 1764 this parish had 162 houses, 173 families, and 1,056 people, more than either of the other three parishes. In 1740 Mr. Shaw built what is still known as the Shaw house, where he fitted boys for college and young men for the ministry. His son, Dr. Samuel Shaw, the doctor of the parish, occupied it afterward; and then a grandson, John A. Shaw, the famous teacher, who added the broad roof and the tower, and lived there till his death in 1874.

During the eighteenth century all the country towns were quiet farming towns. The scattered houses were mostly low, brown cottages, and probably some of the primitive log houses still remained. The name of "city," which is still given to a small group of houses in the south-west of the town, seems to have originated in the building of some two-storied houses there, which the neighbors said was getting "rather citified." In the present village the Shaw, Edson, Withington, and Washburn houses, and a part of the Revere house, are all that survive from the last century. There were probably very few buildings near the meeting-house and the store, besides these houses. Even as late as 1810 there were barely a dozen houses in this village. The Edson house was probably built by Joseph Leonard, on the old Leonard farm, soon after 1700, and is the oldest building in the village. Soon after 1732 Colonel Josiah Edson occupied it. He was a Tory; and, when the Revolution broke out, he went to Boston. His property was confiscated in 1783, and was bought by Isaac Lazell, afterward known as Major, who lived in the Edson house. With his brother Nathan, who lived in what is now a part of the Revere house, he kept the store for many years. With them the Lazell family first appeared here. The Withington house on South Street, now occupied by Mr. Avery F. Hooper, was built before 1765. The Washburn house (seen on the left-hand foreground of the upper picture of Summer Street), now Mr. O. B. Cole's, was built about 1776 by Captain Abraham Washburn, an officer in the Revolutionary War, and stands on the original John Washburn farm, now covered by the village east of South Street and the Common. There are but three of the name who still retain any portion of it,— Mr. Clinton Washburn and sister, and Miss Hannah A. Washburn, who lives opposite the old family home, and who has contributed this account: "In 1716 John Washburn and his wife Rebecca (great-grand-parents of the Revolutionary Captain Abraham) gave the land for the old graveyard, the Unitarian church, and the beautiful green in front of it. They are both buried near the western corner of the graveyard. Most of the old large trees in town were set out by Colonel Abram (grandson of Captain Abraham), who brought two hundred of them, when very small, from Vermont in his chaise-box. They are mostly maple and ash, with a few bass. Those who love the white water-lily, which is so abundant in Carver's Pond, will like to know that it was planted there by Colonel Abram. The roots were brought by him from Halifax Pond. He gave to the State the half of the present Normal grounds that fronts on School Street. There have been two governors of the name of Washburn, who were descendants of this family; and the three Washburn brothers who were in Congress at the same time also trace their ancestry to the same source."

The only manufacturing in this century was the iron business, on the site of the present Iron Works, begun in a small way in 1707, where David Perkins had previously opened a blacksmith's shop and built a dam in the river; but the business declined till the time of the Revolution, when it rapidly increased.

Early in Mr. Shaw's ministry the parish lost a good deal of its membership by the organization of the Titicut Parish in 1743, when the south-west part of the South Parish was joined to a part of Middleboro, the meeting-house being in North Middleboro. This was a consequence of the "New Light" controversy, following the famous revival all through New England in 1740, which was called the "great awakening." The preaching of Whitefield and his friends, and of Edwards, Hopkins, and Bellamy, had made a deep impression, and led to much discussion. The Old Lights were the conservative party, who wished to maintain the old laws of the State which enforced church attendance, taxed every one for the support of the parish ministers, and gave special privileges to them; this party favored the old-fashioned religious methods also. The New Lights were the radicals of their time, who aimed at a complete separation of Church and State by a voluntary system of church support, such as was finally adopted in 1836, favored the new revival methods, and urged the employment of any successful preachers, even though not college-educated, as the parish clergy always were at that time.

Iron Works Bell.

In 1756 Solomon Reed was ordained parish minister of Titicut, and served twenty-eight years, till his death in 1785. David Gurney succeeded him from 1787 to 1815, and Philip Colby from 1817 to 1851. In 1823 the part of the Titicut parish which originally belonged to Bridgewater was reunited.

In 1788 Zedekiah Sanger, afterward made a Doctor of Divinity, was called from his settlement in Duxbury, and installed as colleague to Mr. Shaw, who died three years later. He was minister for thirty-two years, till his death in 1820, at the age of seventy-two. He lived in a house on Plymouth Street, which is now Mr. Stetson's farm-house, and where now the corner of Spring Street is. Like Mr. Shaw, he educated young men for college and for the ministry. His salary was $400 and twenty cords of wood. For two years he was master of the Academy, built in 1799, on the site of the present Inn, with a yard extending where the lower part of the Common now is. Dr. Sanger's ministry, beginning just after the Revolution and continuing for several years after the War of 1812, saw the development of this parish from a quiet farming community to an important manufacturing and educational centre. In 1783 the Iron Works had revived, under the energetic management of the Lazells. In 1802 a second store, now Crane & Burrill's, was opened by Edward Mitchell and others where there had been a blacksmith's shop, opposite the first store. In 1805-6, chiefly by the influence of General Sylvanus Lazell of East Bridgewater, the Boston and New Bedford turnpike was laid out, passing through what are now Broad and Bedford Streets, which were then opened; and this parish was thus placed in the direct line of all travel and business between these two important sea-coast towns, lying about half-way. In 1810 this parish had 1,234 people, an increase of only 177 people in forty-six years. The large and continuous emigration to Western Massachusetts, New Hampshire, and Vermont, and afterward to Maine, accounts for this. But in 1815 the iron business became prosperous here, especially after the railroad was opened in 1846; and till 1870 it continued so, very much enriching the town. Business and population increased; and when the North, West, and East Parishes were set apart and incorporated as towns, in 1821-23, this parish inherited the name and traditions of the ancient town, and, as Bridgewater, it began to take on its present aspect. Hitherto the town was not only thinly settled, but also bare of shade-trees; but from this time and especially about 1847, largely by the influence of Williams Latham, the present trees, which make our streets remarkably beautiful, were set out. The present Inn was built in 1827 by Captain Abram Washburn. The third story was added in 1846. It was kept for a while by Captain Asa Pratt, who since about 1800 had kept the Pratt tavern, to which he soon returned, though he no longer kept it as a tavern. This was at the head of Pleasant Street, on the road to Scotland, built about 1779, and was long a popular place of resort from all parts of the town. The last remnant was taken down in 1898. In 1822 the Common was laid out, but was not fenced in for a while; and the second Academy was built on the present site, the land being given by the heirs of Major Isaac Lazell. It was taken down in 1868, and replaced by the third Academy (see the picture of the "old Academy"), which was enlarged in 1898 to its present shape.

Part of the Pratt Tavern.

In 1821 Richard Manning Hodges was ordained as the fourth minister of the old parish, and resigned in 1833. Soon after he was settled here, in 1823, he abolished the old-time custom of the congregation rising and standing when the minister came in and went out. During Dr. Sanger's ministry nearly all the families in the parish attended the old church; and the only other place of worship was the original Episcopal church near the Iron Works, which had been built in 1748, the services being held irregularly till the church was thoroughly renovated in 1816, and the congregation being small till 1831. But in 1821 the "Trinitarian Congregational Church" in Scotland was formed, and the first Swedenborgian services were held in the old "Number Six" school-house, which led to the organization of the present New Church Society in 1824; and thus it happened that in the first year of Mr. Hodges' ministry the parish unity was broken. In 1836 a new Episcopal church, near the Iron Works, and the Central Square church were built, the latter by the Scotland society, a majority of whom transferred the organization to the central village and left the minority to reorganize in Scotland. In this same year the privileges of the old parish societies were swept away throughout the State by the popular vote and the legislative action, adopting the voluntary system and putting all religious societies on an equality, and the heirs of the property and traditions of the old parishes became the First Parishes, or the First Congregational Societies; and in the three Bridgewaters to-day these are in Unitarian fellowship.

In 1824 the Plymouth County Agricultural Society, organized in 1819, located its permanent exhibition here, and in 1855 bought the sixty acres which have been known since as the Fair Grounds, and where exhibitions have been given yearly.

In 1833 Theophilus P. Doggett was ordained, the fifth and last minister of the parish under the old order of things. He served till 1844.

In 1840 the Normal School was opened here, of which an account is given in another chapter. In 1842 the Mount Prospect Cemetery was dedicated. In 1843 the present Town Hall was built.

The first New Church house of worship was dedicated in 1834, the present house in 1871. The old house was hired by the Methodist society in 1874, who bought it in 1879 and remodelled it in 1894. The present Unitarian church was built in 1845; the present Central Square church in 1862, remodelled in 1883; the present Episcopal church in 1883, the Catholic church in 1855, enlarged in 1898.

In 1846 the railroad from Boston was built, and another railroad from Fall River. From this time the town grew rapidly. In 1830 the population was 1,855, a gain of 621 in twenty years, largely due to the reuniting of Titicut with this town; but in 1865 it was 4,196; in 1895, 4,686; and since then has considerably increased.

Various manufactures were established here during this century: in 1823 the paper-mill at Pratt-town, where there had been a dam in 1792, a grist-mill in 1794, and a fulling-mill in 1798; in 1823 the Eagle Cotton-gin Works, established by Bates, Hyde & Co., in 1846 moved to the present site, and rebuilt in 1853 after a fire; in 1848 the Perkins Iron Foundry; and about 1870 the first shoe factory.

In 1853 the State Farm was established here, of which an account is given in another chapter. In 1872 the Bridgewater Savings Bank was incorporated. In 1876 Henry T. Pratt opened a printing-office, and published a twelve-column weekly, the *Every Saturday*, which in December was enlarged, and took the name of the *Independent*. It was published by Mr. Pratt till 1880, when it passed into other hands and is still published here. It is interesting to know that Bridgwater in England also has its weekly *Independent*. In 1882 the Memorial Library was finished. In 1887 the town water-works were built. In 1897–99 the electric cars connected this town with East and West Bridgewater, Brockton, Taunton, Middleboro, and through them with all the outlying world. Within recent years many new streets have been laid out, numerous residences built, and the loveliness of our town has drawn many families here to make their permanent homes with us.

A Common Weed

I FIND it growing here and there
  In many places far away
From that, so dear and pleasant, where
  I first beheld its mean array.

Oft have I asked what name it bears,
  But none is wise enough to tell;
"Only a common weed;" it wears
  That modest blazon passing well.

No shame it ever seems to take,
  Whatever company it keeps;
Nor — vagabond of flowers — to make
  The least ado where'er it sleeps.

It has no beauty to desire,
  Gives, leaf nor bloom, no pleasant smell;
Yet are there flowers which I admire,
  But do not love one-half so well.

And why, but that when I was small,—
  A little boy of summers few,—
Beside a ruddy cottage wall
  This common weed so blithely grew

As if it were the fairest rose
  That ever on the breast of June
Made sweetness there: so from it flows
  A spell that puts my heart in tune

With all the poor, pathetic things
  Of that young life so long ago,
And from their shape and action brings
  A kindling warmth, a kindly glow.

I see again the tiny yard
  That neighbored with the open door;
The narrow plot of feeble sward;
  Within, the spotless yellow floor.

And, moving softly to and fro,
  My mother with her gentle eyes,
My father bronzed as those who go
  Down to the sea in ships, and wise

In all its lore, my sisters dear,—
  I seem to see them now as then;
And, as the present moment clear,
  All their young ways come back again.

Nor these alone, but all that made
  My early years so warm and bright
That heaven's self might cheaply fade,
  Matched with such simple-sweet delight.

Such magic has this common weed
  To charm my backward-yearning heart
That I would plant its fruitful seed
  E'en where the "skyey roadways" part.

And just because you have the power
  To work this miracle for me,
Poor little, nameless, graceless flower,
  I love you very tenderly.

JOHN WHITE CHADWICK.

RECOLLECTIONS OF BRIDGEWATER.

Y recollections of Bridgewater are those of my early youth, and naturally touched with the glamour that hangs about that time. The people that I then knew are remembered by many besides me. There were some striking figures among them. Mr. Nicholas Tillinghast was principal of the Normal School, which was then not far from its beginning. He was the animating spirit of the school, impressing upon it his own strong individuality. Tall, quiet, and reserved to people in general, he gave the idea of coldness; but those who came under his charge, who worked with him, or knew him intimately, knew the force and fervor which he carried into his work and into his life, making him a power and an inspiration.

The Hon. John A. Shaw was an important man in his own character, his scholarly life, and well-considered opinions. He also represented the family of the old minister, the second in Bridgewater, and so gathered to himself much of the respect which was in olden times so surely paid to the minister. He himself studied for the ministry, but gave it up after a few years' service in the pulpit. He spent so many years in New Orleans as Superintendent of Public Schools that he seemed almost like a visitor to his native town. Still, he had for many years in Bridgewater a boys' school; and there are men now living who were his pupils, and remember him and Mrs. Shaw with affectionate respect.

Dr. Nahum Washburn was *the* dentist, *par excellence*, of all the country round. He had great skill for those days, and so much common (or uncommon) sense that he anticipated much of the success achieved in later times in his profession. His wit and genial manners made him so interesting that it was often said that Dr. Washburn was so agreeable that his patients were unaware of pain or discomfort.

Perhaps the most prominent man in Bridgewater in those days was the Hon. Artemas Hale. He had represented the town and district for so long a time that he seemed to stand always as the typical political man. He was simple, straightforward, with no pretence, full of activity and zeal for the best interests of his town and country. I can see him now, a small, plain figure, running along the streets, full of business. Some one spoke of his lack of dignity,— that he ran instead of walking in a sedate manner; and I well remember the answer made to this remark,— that Mr. Hale's dignity was in his character.

There was Captain Abram Washburn, a very old man as I remember him. He seemed to have come out of the far past, with its imprint on him, as if he were a link to bind us to the times and people that were gone. He was somewhat gruff to us children, but he could not so hide from us a certain friendliness to our youth and wildness.

There were our two good doctors, Dr. Pratt, our friendly neighbor, and Dr. Samuel Alden, who with his descent from John and Priscilla, the immortal Pilgrim lovers, inherited the quaint wit that distinguishes the family. Skilful and sympathetic, his warm feelings were partly expressed and partly veiled by his keen and witty remarks.

There were many other notable people whom I could name; but, in the short article I am to write, I will add only Colonel Abram Washburn. To my youthful imagination he was the incarnation of the Spirit of '76. I never thought of the Revolutionary patriot except as being like Colonel Washburn. Tall and straight, brave and simple, stern, but gentle, he seemed to be the true American citizen. He threw himself heart and soul into the cause of anti-slavery. As he was closely bound to my father by this common interest, they made a station, as it were, on the Underground Railroad. There were secrets in those stormy days, to be carefully kept; but I well remember when Colonel Washburn called us into his house to see the afterward famous William and Ellen Crafts, then fugitives from captivity. Every one knew their story later. They were husband and wife; but the wife, being fair, took the character of a young planter, while her husband attended her as a slave servant. These parts were so well carried out that they made the steamer passage successfully, and eluded pursuit. Afterward they travelled abroad, and were much fêted and admired.

Then there was William Box Brown, as he was called, a large and stalwart man, who had himself packed into a small box, and sent as freight to the North. Being forgotten or mis-sent somewhere, he had to pass some days in a curled-up position, frightful to think of, sometimes head down. How he survived to tell the tale was a wonder to all.

Colonel Washburn lived long after those troublous times, to see all the slaves free, surviving, I think, all the others I have named and most of his family and generation. He lived beloved and died lamented, to be ever tenderly remembered by those who knew him.

LUCIA ALDEN BRADFORD KNAPP.

(From a private letter.)

I was to board at Philo Mitchell's on the Scotland road, which ran off into the open country from our door, inviting me to follow it; and many a time I did. Just below us toward the village was the Rev. David Brigham's parsonage. His daughter was a lovely saint; and, when she died, what Dante said of Beatrice seemed true of her,—

> "No quality of cold nor yet of heat
> Robbed us of her as it of others does.
> But her supreme benignity alone."

Some of her own verses I remember, and sometimes I repeat them when standing by a new-made grave.

The Rev. John Jay Putnam was then the Unitarian minister at Bridgewater, and I preached my first sermon in his pulpit. He objected, I remember, to the way I tossed my hat upon the pulpit sofa, and told me how that function should have been performed. The Rev. Theodore Rodman, the Swedenborgian minister, was very friendly to me, and, without my knowledge, wrote James Freeman Clarke that I had the making of a minister in me. He was an ardent Emersonian and had a beautiful and well-instructed mind.

Much more I should like to write,— of Mr. Conant and Mr. Boyden and Miss Woodward — how kind she was to me! and of Alfred Bunker, my room-mate, and Will Grover,— they tell me he is dead,— the splendid beauty of whose face and form enraptured my young heart, and of —— and —— and ——. They are all grandmothers now, but then ——! Plainly, it is time to bring this letter to a close.

JOHN WHITE CHADWICK.

SON-LATELL WASHBURN HOUSE

NEW ACADEMY

RIVER AT FAIR GROUNDS

SUMNER ST.

AT SCHOOL: FROM FOUR TO SIXTEEN.

T was in the spring of one of the forties — the curious may learn the exact year by consulting the town records and then performing a mental calculation — when a certain little girl, having attained the age of four years, was considered fit to set forth in pursuit of knowledge. Accordingly, armed with Worcester's Primer and a small slate to which a pencil was tied,— for no kind town then furnished our weapons of attack,— she entered the small building on Cedar Street near the present Methodist church, then occupied by the New Jerusalem Society. The old school-house now faces School Street; and, by being raised and enlarged, it was long since converted into a dwelling-house.

In that small building of only one room besides the entries, gathered all the pupils from four years of age upward, in district number one, who attended public school. To this child reading came by nature, as Dogberry averred it comes to all, so that in the course of a week after entering school she was promoted to the Second Book. How many now remember the thrilling story of Peggy Hammond, and the dire mishaps following her fear of spiders and other creeping things? It must have been about this time that the whole class were condemned to stand in the floor until they could master the combination of letters in the word "ache." To how high a grade must a pupil now attain before he can spell the word? "Thieves" was another word which conquered the child. But she never forgot it after the noon when she had to remain after school to learn it. In those days, few of the small children attended the common school in winter. Perhaps it would have been hardly safe during the time when the master was accustomed to throw ferules and jack-knives across the room at disorderly pupils. A man was always hired for the winter, so that there was generally a new teacher for every term.

But the education of young children was not neglected during the winter and the long vacations. Several young ladies stood ready to open private schools, tuition being ninepence a week.

A popular school was held in the little yellow building owned by Colonel Washburn which stood at the left of the present Methodist church. There were no desks, but shelves or corner brackets served as receptacles for books and work and for refractory pupils too. Consternation was caused one day when a girl who had stretched out on her shelf rolled off to the floor. And imagine the stately Miss —— perched on a bracket when visitors arrived!

With short terms at the town school eked out by private instruction, our girl struggled on for four years, reading, writing, spelling, studying Mitchell's Primary Geography, Emerson's Arithmetic for Beginners, followed by Colburn's First Steps in Numbers. Then a change was made, and the most advanced of the pupils were put into the Model School of the first Normal Building. The teacher was an admirable one, loved and respected by all; and many now living can testify to the good influences, mental and moral, of Miss L.

After a year in the Normal Building there was another change, and both common-school grades were housed on the first floor of the old Academy. There they remained until the spring of 1852, when the magnificent edifice, removed a few years ago to make room for the new Normal School, was opened. But before its destruction it had taken on wings and was quite different from its original form, when it contained only three school-rooms. The first winter in the new house the teacher was a man who confessed his inability to teach and govern at the same time. So his method was to impart knowledge for a while, and then to stop and call to the floor pupils enough to form a line across the room, when he severely feruled the whole row. As all were conscious of meriting punishment, it was quite exciting to listen and hear if one's name was called. Our girl escaped, perhaps owing to certain red apples bestowed daily upon the wielder of the ferule. His successor was a lady, who proved so popular that, when she went to become assistant at the Academy, many of the pupils went with her, our young friend among them.

How funny it was there! Sometimes the school was on the second floor, sometimes on the first. Sometimes the boys were in the room one side of the hall and the girls in the other, sometimes all were condensed into one. Sometimes there was an assistant, and sometimes pupils went to a neighboring house to recite certain branches. How impressive were the annual visits of the trustees, grave and reverend men from half the towns in the county! They assembled at the hotel, and then marched to the Academy. It would require some time for them to become seated, as only a few could be accommodated on the lofty platform; and each, with profound bows, would insist that his neighbor must have the honor.

At the time of which I write, the principal's chair was most of the time occupied by a veteran schoolmaster, who remained in town so many years as to be well remembered now. His ways were peculiar, but had much of good in them. He required pupils to make obeisance to him upon entering or leaving the school-room. He claimed that it was an act of respect to the position he occupied, and that in his absence his chair represented him, so that the pupils were expected to bow profoundly to that piece of furniture when it was vacant. Perhaps some did. His strong point was his requiring pupils to memorize, *verbatim et literatim et punctuatim*. Well, one's head may be filled with worse stuff than volumes of Latin or English Grammar. Probably there are several in town who could recite in concert the "poetry" commencing, "About, above, across." Then there were the sweet lines beginning "Ad, ante, con," and "A, ab or abs, absque," and "Ad, adversum or adversus." He made presents of time for various perfectly recited tasks. The twenty-six prepositions governing the accusative gained an hour's freedom from school. Offences were atoned for by time, so that he had a debit and credit account with many pupils.

When in after years the hard, dry facts had become digested and assimilated in the mind of our girl, they gave her great strength; and she has never ceased to be glad that she was obliged to learn so much "by heart." Over these days the pen lingers, and much might be written. Gone are all but one of the old school-houses, gone are most of those who there received instruction; but there are ghosts which still wander and sometimes stir the chords of memory. The new times are better, but the old were not wholly bad.

The Normal School and its past work are so well known that we leave our girl on its threshold at sixteen.

MARTHA KEITH.

LIBRARY   PLEASANT ST

SOUTH ST

THE MEMORIAL LIBRARY.

SO many libraries in our towns have been created by the gifts of individuals who have gone out from them and gained wealth, and then returned to show their affection for the old home, that a stranger, looking upon our substantial building, might expect to find some person's name upon its portal. But the names here are the names of patriotic men who served their country and died for it, and the library is from the beginning until now a child of the whole town.

When the Rev. Zedekiah Sanger, D.D., was pastor of the First Church from 1788 to 1820, his home was a seat of learning. Besides his ten children, he had in his family students for college and the ministry; and what wonder is it that he should have become a subscriber for the great book of the day, Rees' Cyclopedia! But the salary of four hundred dollars was outstripped by the encyclopedia of eighty-seven volumes; and at last a general subscription gave the book broad ownership. This was the beginning. An excellent library of choice literature was later owned by a company of ladies, and libraries were developed to some degree in the school districts; and thus a town library was but a step beyond, especially when the Hon. Artemas Hale offered a number of valuable books.

In 1879 the library began in a hired room with about three thousand books, in charge of Miss Lydia L. Lewis. The first report of the trustees in 1880 shows no book lost, eleven thousand books loaned, and a fair use of the reading-room. As was hoped for, this good beginning led the way to the erection by the town, with some gifts by individuals and everybody's help in some way or other, of a building; and no idea could so appropriately have given form to this object as that of a Soldiers' Memorial.

The first movement for the Memorial made no mention of its form, however, as was the wisest course while everything was uncertain; but an earnest meeting was held in the Town Hall October 1, 1879, and a plan of organization was then adopted. The Library Trustees and the Memorial Committee worked together from the start; and in the month of December, 1880, a bazaar was held, in which every section of the town was fully represented. The hall was crowded for three days. The receipts were $1,110.35 and the expenses $23.80, leaving $1,086.55 as the nucleus of the Memorial Fund.

At its annual meeting in March, 1881, the town voted "to proceed at once to erect a building commemorating the patriotism of our citizens in time of national peril, and providing a suitable hall for the public library and for such objects of historic and scientific interest as may come into possession of the town." A committee was then raised to report on plan, location, and cost. This committee reported a month later. A discussion arose over the site, but was amicably settled; and all proceedings moved without delay to the completion of the building. Thirty-six names appeared on the tablets.

The dedication took place on Memorial Day, 1882, with a procession and exercises at the building and in the Central Square Church. Every word spoken was appropriate, and all felt that a good deed had been done by them that day. The expense of the building was $14,481.19, of which the town appropriated $9,057.15; and the rest came from other sources, of which $848.96 was the amount of the unexpected balance of the Soldiers' Fund raised by the women of the town during the Civil War.

The fourth annual report of the Library Trustees expresses satisfaction with the new building, gives the number of books as 4,217, shows a largely increased circulation, and speaks especially of the museum as well established by means of numerous donations. Miss Lucia L. Christian was then librarian, and has continued to be wholly faithful to this responsible position. Except to mention the two excellent librarians, I have refrained from mentioning names of those still in this life; but, when I was lately asked if I knew one George H. Martin, now of Boston, my mind ran back to him as chairman of the first committee to organize the Memorial Fund. And, certainly, scores of us knew each other well in those days, and took great happiness in working together.

I shall always believe that the great satisfaction experienced by all who were instrumental in bringing the library and its building into existence, and in guiding its growth to the present time, was due to the unusually high average intelligence of the town. Books were appreciated by all or almost all, as is evident from the smaller libraries already in existence in churches and schools. The old Academy should have the credit of this, as far as those were concerned who directly or indirectly benefited by its classical instruction; but perhaps a more pervasive influence had emanated from the Normal School since its establishment in 1840. A person who should go through the town would find that almost every teacher was a Normal graduate, and was in close touch with his or her Alma Mater, and thus was deeply interested in learning and imparting the knowledge which is power. There was, therefore, a degree of eagerness for a public library; and this was especially felt by the teachers, who from the beginning have been accorded special privileges and have made excellent use of them by introducing their scholars to the best and most appropriate reading.

Before we had the library, a farmer, who had been kept at home by illness, was asked what he had done to employ his time. "Well, I read my Bible and my weekly paper," said in a tone which implied that he had found the winter a long one. Now a good book each week between the Bible and the newspaper satisfied him completely. One man about ninety years of age immediately laid out for himself a course of reading, taking Africa for his subject, and became an authority on that continent and on the explorations from Mungo Park to Stanley.

Some of the present trustees were among the most active workers from the start. They and the whole town deserve to be congratulated on the completion in 1898 of the beautiful catalogue, showing some eleven thousand volumes, a yearly use of twenty-five thousand, five thousand cards issued to patrons, three thousand books loaned in the schools, the museum still growing, friends still contributing time and money, and everything accomplished that was in the minds of the pioneers except an endowment. This should not now be far away. If the library could now be endowed by some donor or donors, it would be better off than if it had received it twenty years ago; but now it needs just this access of strength. The library has grown like a tree planted by the rivers of waters, and it has brought forth its fruit in its season.

THEODORE F. WRIGHT.

THE STATE NORMAL SCHOOL.

HIS school is one of the first three State normal schools on this continent. The Hon. Edmund Dwight, of Boston, offered to furnish $10,000, "to be expended under the direction of the Board of Education for qualifying teachers for our common schools," on condition that the legislature would appropriate for the same purpose an equal amount. On the 19th of April, 1838, the legislature passed a resolve accepting this offer. The board decided to establish three schools for the education of teachers, each to be continued three years, as an experiment, and on May 30, 1838, voted to establish one of these schools in the county of Plymouth. On December 28, 1838, the board voted to establish the other two at Lexington and Barre. Prominent men in Plymouth County, of whom Artemas Hale of Bridgewater was chief, spent two years in the endeavor to raise $10,000 for the erection of new buildings for the school. The towns of Abington, Wareham, Plymouth, Duxbury, and Marshfield, voted to make appropriations for the school, from the surplus revenue which had just before been divided by the general government. After vigorous competition it was decided to locate the school at Bridgewater, whereupon some of the towns refused to redeem their pledges, and the funds were not realized. Bridgewater granted to the school the free use of its town hall for three years, and the next three years the school paid a rental of $50 a year. Here, by the skill and genius of its first principal, Nicholas Tillinghast, the experiment of a State normal school in the Old Colony was successfully performed. In 1846, the State, with the liberal co-operation of the town of Bridgewater and its citizens, provided a permanent home for the school. The school was opened September 9, 1840, with a class of 28 pupils, 7 men and 21 women.

It has had only three principals: Nicholas Tillinghast, who served from 1840 to 1853; Marshall Conant, who served from 1853 to 1860; and Albert G. Boyden, since 1860.

The first six years of its life the school held its sessions in the town hall. In 1846 it moved into a new building, the first State Normal School Building erected in America. In 1861 this building was enlarged, increasing its capacity 70 per cent. In 1871 this building was increased 50 per cent. by adding a third story. In 1881 a building for chemical, physical, and industrial laboratories was built. In 1890 these buildings were removed and a massive brick structure, 86 feet in front by 187 feet in length, three stories above the basement, was erected. In 1894 this building was extended, increasing its capacity 50 per cent. In 1869 the boarding department of the school became a necessity; and a residence hall was erected, accommodating 52 students and the family of the principal. In 1873 it was enlarged to accommodate 148 students. In 1891 the laboratory building was converted into a residence hall, accommodating 32 students. In 1895 Tillinghast Hall was erected with accommodations for 72 students. The present school building, with its equipments, is not surpassed by any normal school building in the country in its adaptation to its purpose. It will accommodate 275 normal students and a practice school of 500 pupils. The grounds have been increased from one and one-quarter acres to sixteen acres, including a beautiful park and grove of six and one-half acres and a field of two acres for athletic sports.

The course of required studies was three successive terms of fourteen weeks up to

March, 1855. From this time to March, 1865, it was three successive terms of twenty weeks each. Since March, 1865, the shorter course required has been four successive terms of twenty weeks each. In 1870 the four years' course was established. At the present time five courses are in operation: a two years' course, a three years', a four years', a kindergarten course, and a special course for graduates of colleges and normal schools and for teachers who have had five years' experience in teaching.

In the beginning there was a model school in connection with the normal school, composed of children of the neighborhood who were to be taught by the normal pupils under the eye and direction of their teachers.

This school was kept the first six years in a small school-house near the normal school, erected for the purpose by the centre school district of the town. Afterward the school was kept in the model school-room in the normal school-house.

Practice teaching was not very attractive to the normal pupils, and some parents preferred that their children should not be "experimented with." Mr. Tillinghast was quite willing that the school should be discontinued. It was closed in March, 1850.

From 1880 to 1891 the primary grades of the centre school were used by the normal school as a school of observation. In September, 1891, the whole centre school came into the new normal school building, to be used as a school for observation and practice by the normal school. The State provides the building and the supplies for the school, and pays part of the salaries of the teachers. Its purpose is to exemplify the mode of conducting a good public school and to train the normal students in observing and teaching children. It is under the general supervision of the principal of the normal school, the direct supervision of the vice-principal, and includes the kindergarten and the nine elementary grades of the public school of the centre of the town. It has twelve teachers, — a principal and a regular teacher for each grade, and a supervisor of the practice of the normal students. The number enrolled in the model school is 440.

The whole number of pupils admitted to the school has been 1,263 men, 3,360 women; total, 4,623. The whole number of graduates has been 817 men, 2,064 women; total, 2,881. The number of graduates from the four years' course has been 128 men, 113 women; total, 241.

The school has sought to set before its students a high ideal of what life should be, to awaken the conscience to the responsibilities of the teacher, to give them command of themselves, of the philosophy of teaching, of the subjects to be used in teaching, and such a knowledge of children that they shall be able to practise the art of teaching in the education of their pupils.

The school has a national reputation. Its graduates are engaged in all lines of educational work, — as teachers in common, high, and normal schools, as superintendents of schools, State agents, and State superintendents. Some have become prominent as lawyers, physicians, clergymen, and in business. Many as wives and mothers exert a strong educational influence. Some are missionaries. The influence of the school is felt around the globe.

ALBERT G. BOYDEN.

NOTE. — The views of the front and rear of Normal Hall, which were taken in 1881, as given in the plate, show it as it still is. The Grammar School was removed in 1891, and Tillinghast Hall stands nearly on the site of it. Woodward Hall was originally part of the Normal School Building, and in 1891 was removed to its present site behind Normal Hall.

PARISH AND CHURCH IN THE OLD TIMES.

HE leaders in the settlement of Salem in 1628, and later of Boston and other towns in the Massachusetts Bay Colony, were non-conformists, who were willing to stay in the English "Established" National Church, if certain teachings and ritual forms could be modified, which tended, as they thought, toward the Catholic Church. They refused to conform to these customs and to assent to these teachings; and, therefore, they were persecuted in England and their ministers forced out of the pulpits of the Church. They were called Puritans because they wished to purify the doctrine and worship of the National Church. The Pilgrims, on the other hand, who settled in Plymouth in 1620, were "Separatists," or "Independents," who objected to any kind of "establishment" or support of religious institutions by the civil government, and would have every religious society entirely independent of all others with regard to creed and worship. They wanted to separate entirely from the National Church. The Puritans of Massachusetts Bay were, therefore, somewhat aristocratic in their ideas of religious institutions, as in many of their social customs: whereas the Pilgrims were thoroughly democratic. Between the non-conformist and the Pilgrim ideas there began, then, a struggle which really lasted for more than two hundred years till 1836, when the Pilgrim ideas finally conquered and the voluntary system of supporting religious institutions was legally introduced.

From the very first the ideas of the non-conformists in Salem and Boston were modified by the peculiar circumstances of their life in this New World, and they soon ceased to consider themselves members of the Church of England. They adopted from time to time some of the Separatist ideas, and thus formed the distinctive Congregationalism of Massachusetts. But they could not for a long time break away from certain convictions about the duty of the civil government to support religious institutions by compelling towns to settle ministers, enforcing attendance at public worship, and requiring payment of taxes for the expense of these institutions, which is called the union of Church and State,—convictions which had been universally held in Christendom for many centuries, and were unanimously held in the time of the Puritans by all but some insignificant sects, like the Separatists and the Quakers. They, therefore, tried to organize an "Established Church" here, in which the governor and legislature would control all ecclesiastical affairs, just as Parliament and the bishops did in England, and only the members of their Puritan churches should vote or hold office in town and State, just as in England only Episcopal church-members were allowed these privileges. The Puritans had been the dissenters in England, but here they treated all other people as dissenters.

The Puritans had been in Massachusetts Bay but three years, when they enacted in 1631 that "no one shall be admitted to the freedom of this body politic"— that is, shall be allowed to vote or hold office — "unless he be a member of some church "— that is, of some church duly authorized by the legislature —" within the limits of the same"; and this law was enforced till 1664. But it was also enacted in 1638 that all inhabitants, whether church-members or not, should be taxed for church expenses as well as for town expenses, except in Boston, where for some reason pew-owners only were taxed for church support. In the Plymouth Colony, however, all "heads of families" were allowed to vote, because the Pilgrims did not believe in uniting Church and State and giving the church-members entire control of the civil government. The Massachusetts Colony was thus organized after the English model; and in 1646 it re-enacted the English law compelling church attendance, and required a fine of five shillings for each absence without good cause on the Lord's Day, Fast Day, or Thanksgiving,— a very heavy fine for those times. It was regarded by the common law of England as a penal offence not to attend church. In 1647 the rigor of the law of 1631 was somewhat relaxed by a law allowing others than church-members to vote for selectmen and on tax questions, but still refusing them the privilege of voting for State officers.

The governor and legislature, thus chosen by church-members, had great authority. They could remove heretical or vicious ministers and aid feeble churches. After 1650 they passed laws requiring every town to be supplied with a minister, meeting-house, and parsonage, and to tax all land-owners for religious expenses. The County Court was authorized to enforce these laws. In 1651 the Malden church was fined by the legislature for not consulting the other churches and the legislature in choosing a minister, and churches often petitioned the legislature to find ministers for them.

But this state of things was possible only while Cromwell and the Puritans governed England. In 1662, soon after the accession of Charles II. to the throne, the royal command came to make all English land-owners voters in State affairs, "if of competent estate"; and in 1664 the Massachusetts legislature reluctantly yielded, making the payment of ten shillings tax a condition of having the privilege of voting. Thus the old theocracy of church-members, which had ruled the State for thirty-three years, came to an end. Still, the churches, though losing control of the civil government, retained till 1780, more than a century, the privilege of choosing the ministers whom the people were taxed to support. But after 1692, when the colonial charter had been taken away and Massachusetts became a royal province under a governor appointed by the king, the churches consulted the non-church-members in town-meetings about the settlement of ministers. In this year, too, the Plymouth Colony became part of the Province of Massachusetts and was governed by Massachusetts laws.

Previous to this date the words "parish" and "precinct" do not occur in the records; but in the provincial times they came into use as indiscriminate names for "town," or gradually as names for a town in its relation to the church for which it voted and raised money. Pretty early it became convenient to have two or more meeting-houses in different parts of a town; and then the town was divided territorially into as many parishes or precincts, and their bounds were exactly defined by the legislature. Thus in Bridgewater the South Parish was "set off" in 1716; the East Parish, in 1723, what remained being called the West Parish; in 1738, the North Parish; and in 1743, the Titicut Parish.

But now a new complication arose. During the eighteenth century there grew up new religious societies within these territorial parishes, and the supporters of these new movements felt it to be a grievance that they should still be compelled to pay taxes for the support of the parish minister also. A long agitation followed. As early as 1728 Quakers were exempted from the "minister's tax." In Boston and a few other places it was never enforced or was early abolished. In other places, as early as 1735, town treasurers were ordered to pay to the Episcopal rectors their parishioners' minister's tax, provided these parishioners brought certain certificates. The Baptists obtained some relief in 1757, and the Universalists in 1786. The Methodists first appear about 1790. But in 1754 the legislature had enacted that any town or parish, if so disposed, could adopt the Boston custom of taxing only pew-owners in the parish church. In 1791 the old fine of five shillings for every absence was changed to a fine of ten shillings for three months' absence, and this was not repealed till 1835. After 1780 laws were passed allowing people to indicate to what church in the town their minister's taxes should be paid. If no preference was expressed, the taxes went to support the parish minister. But in 1804 the court decided that a minister must be ordained and settled over a society, not merely an itinerant, in order to receive the benefit of the minister's taxes. It had been already decided that a society did not need to be incorporated, and many dissenting societies were formed at this time for the purpose of evading the payment of the minister's tax; but in 1810 it was decided that dissenting societies must be incorporated. In 1811 "the religious freedom act" was passed, practically reversing this by providing that any tax-payer could, on filing a certificate with the town treasurer, have his tax paid to any minister in his town; but until 1831 business corporations were not allowed this privilege; their minister's taxes went to the support of the parish minister. In 1820 the dissenting societies were about a third of all the religious societies in the State. In 1828 the court decided that every one who could not show that he belonged to some other religious society must be regarded as belonging still to the parish society, where his tax must go and where he also had the privilege of voting in parish meetings.

After 1800 the old rigor with regard to church attendance was further relaxed. Those who wished to attend meeting in another town had been "set off," by special act, on individual petition to the legislature. In 1804 it was enacted that in such cases the minister's tax should be paid by the town treasurer to that other town, and in 1824 it was enacted that this liberty should be allowed without special petition to the legislature.

Until 1829 ministers were exempted from taxation, because they were regarded as town officials, and to tax them would be a breach of faith in cutting down their salaries. In 1807 the Supreme Court decided that, in calling a minister, a life settlement was understood, if no limit of years was specified.

With regard to the settlement of ministers and the relations of church and parish, an equal privilege had been gradually conceded as a courtesy by the church to the parish. But at the time of the Revolution, in 1780, the original relation was entirely reversed by the Third Article of the Bill of Rights in the new Constitution of the State, which provided that "the legislature shall, from time to time, authorize and require the several towns, parishes, precincts, and other bodies politic, or religious societies," to support public worship,—thus ignoring the churches and thereby depriving them of all legal authority. A strong argument in favor of this article was the principle that taxation and the right of voting should go together, in Church as well as in State. The article was drawn up by careful lawyers, who dreaded the possibility of some such priestly tyranny as England had suffered from in the previous century. But the fear was groundless, and the result calamitous. For it gave the religious interests of our towns at that time entirely into the control of the voters of the towns, and many of these voters were often ready to antagonize any moral or religious movement which the minister or the church might try to promote. Even after 1836, when this article was modified so as to abolish all State control, the precedents it established have continued in many cases to degrade the churches, embarrass the pulpits, and seriously injure the religious life of our State, because they have given all legal power to the parish, which might consist of the pew-owners only or be a loosely organized society of people, many of whom have no sympathy with the religious aims of the church. The case of the Rev. John Pierpont, who in 1845 was forced out of the Hollis Street pulpit in Boston on account of his frank preaching on intemperance, was one of many instances. These became so numerous and grievous that in 1887 a statute was passed allowing churches to be incorporated with all the rights of parishes, so as to hold legally their houses of worship and other property, and to have exclusive voice in the settlement and dismissal of ministers. This was a return to the wise spirit of the Puritans, without the injustice of taxing those who have no vote in church affairs. It indicates the path of deliverance from the bondage of the past hundred years and all the mischiefs it has caused. In one large Congregational denomination, all new religious enterprises have been organized as "churches" under this statute; and many old parishes have been induced to surrender their property to the churches connected with them. In many cases, to be sure, there has been perfect harmony between parish and church, and the parishes, as a matter of courtesy, have generally consulted their churches in the settlement of ministers; but where the parish has sole legal authority there is always opportunity for harm to follow in certain contingencies.

Strenuous objections were made to this Third Article at the time of its adoption, especially by the Boston delegates. In 1832 the repeal of it was proposed by the legislature, and in 1834 approved by popular vote, which in 1836 was finally ratified by the legislature, and went into effect April 30. Article XI. of the amendments was substituted, which provides that "all religious sects and denominations shall be equally under the protection of the law, and no subordination of any one sect or denomination to another shall ever be established by law," and also abolishes all taxation by the towns for church support, and leaves to each society absolute freedom in its affairs with no form of State control. A further enactment in 1836, that "no one can be made a member of any religious society without his consent in writing," annulled the decision of the court in 1828, referred to above. The Third Article had been in force for fifty-six years.

The word "parish," about the time of the Revolution, began to be used in a second meaning also; that is, to mean any one of several congregations whose members live in the same territory, or parish, in the old sense. These were often called "poll parishes." And in 1836 the societies which were left in possession of the old parish records, traditions and property, became "poll parishes," like the rest, and were known as First Parishes, because they were the oldest.

Thus for the past sixty-three years the voluntary system of church support has taken the place of the ancient system, which had been the law of Christian Europe for many centuries,— a system which expressed a Christian nation's feeling of responsibility for the religious training of all its people, requiring them all to contribute for the nation's religious institutions and to attend its services. It expressed the same feeling of responsibility for the religious life of the whole nation that our modern common-school system expresses for the mental training of our children, by taxing every citizen according to his means for its support. As long as there was practical harmony of religious thought and feeling, it was easy to maintain this system; for it voiced the nation's deepest faiths and most intense enthusiasms, and support of it was regarded to be as much a patriotic duty as paying taxes for the support of the civil government or taking up arms against a foreign enemy. But the growth of sectarianism made the old system impossible. Yet the consequences of the change have thus far been in some respects deplorable, as is seen in the estrangement of great multitudes from all religious influences, the indifference of most church members to this vast amount of practical paganism right among them, and the shocking waste involved in sectarian rivalries. To meet these new perils, we must devise new methods of religious work under our voluntary system, and awaken a new enthusiasm in our churches, and bring together the sundered sects in a new "unity of the spirit," which will restore religion to its old-time, foremost place in our social and national life, and bring every man, woman, and child under some religious influences.

It is a significant fact that the first settlers of this town organized a church before they formed a civil government. The religious interests of human life were more important to them than the merely material welfare and comfort of life. This was the spirit in which our New England civilization was founded, and only as we are faithful to this spirit can our civilization really prosper.

THE STATE FARM.

HE public institution of the Commonwealth known as the State Farm, a portion of which is represented by the accompanying plate, is not fully shown in character, purpose, or extent by the name given or picture made. The variety of duties required and offices performed in the medical, charitable, and penal directions, precludes for a name any convenient or euphonious word or phrase which would designate clearly the several interests committed by law to its care. The institution originated as a State Almshouse; and the name suggested its sole function then,— that of supporting paupers who were entirely chargeable to the State and hitherto had been aided or supported by towns and cities and reimbursed by the State. So long ago as 1832 this system of State pauper care by the cities and towns was obviously unsatisfactory to the State, and a commission was appointed to investigate the "pauper system" and make recommendations. Various plans of relief and support followed, but the radical change by which the Commonwealth undertook the total support of the unsettled or State paupers in large institutions of their own was not affected till 1853-55. By this time State pauperism had so increased by foreign emigration that the local almshouses were practically swamped by a class who found almshouse conditions in this country luxury as compared with home life in the Old World.

This condition was on, and must be met. The legislature of 1852, in chapter 275, authorized and appropriated therefor $100,000 for three State Almshouses, to accommodate not less than five hundred each. The commission appointed to execute the plan specified, in the "public notice" for locations, "In considering the propositions, the commission will have regard to the centres of the several pauper districts and to the general salubrity and health of the section."

In their report of progress they describe in great detail the selection in South-eastern Massachusetts of the Asahael Shaw farm in Bridgewater. The meagre appropriation for the great undertaking compelled the commission to finally consider nothing more substantial than wooden structures.

May 1, 1855, the almshouse was, by proclamation of his Excellency Governor Emory Washburn, opened under the government of the following officials: Abraham T. Lowe, Bradford L. Wales, and Nahum Stetson, inspectors; Levi L. Goodspeed, superintendent. Evidently, the new order of pauper support was expected to lessen the State's financial burden; and, while the managers were loyal to this principle, they were, nevertheless, convinced that there were other and broader considerations than the dollar and cent cost of a "pauper system."

Herding together more or less indiscriminately by the hundreds, men, women, and children afforded an object-lesson of the social and moral side of the question. A movement for classification soon located the children at Monson, and divided the adults somewhat on disciplinary lines,— the infirm and truly unfortunate at Tewksbury and the voluntary and able-bodied rounders at Bridgewater.

In 1866 the legislature passed an act making this institution also a workhouse, to which could be committed certain so-called vicious paupers. In 1870 Mr. Goodspeed retired after a continuous service of fifteen years, markedly successful. His was the inauguration period, and the unusual duties were discharged with skill and executive power.

As a workhouse, it was natural enough that later legislation should designate it as a place for the commitment of misdemeanor offences; and in 1872 the legislature abolished the name almshouse, but under certain conditions some State paupers could be sent here.

Captain Nahum Leonard, Jr., of Bridgewater, succeeded Mr. Goodspeed as the second superintendent. The State Workhouse had now become practically a penal institution. The appointment of a superintendent possessing Captain Leonard's judicial mind and calm self-possession was now as necessary as had been the push and resolution of his predecessor.

With restricted almshouse liberties came the question of indoor industrial employment. Serious obstacles were met and overcome, and a foundation of industry so firmly laid that the changed name to workhouse was no misnomer.

In 1883, after thirteen years' painstaking care and zealous preservation of this cheaply conceived, poorly constructed old wooden fire-trap, Mr. Leonard resigned, leaving it in far better condition than when he assumed its care.

On July 7, 1883, thirty-six hours after his successor took charge, an incendiary inmate demonstrated that the designation "fire-trap" was quite right by sending up in flame and smoke the huge pile of fuel, in little more time than it takes to tell it. The legislature had not adjourned, but were awaiting the famous "Tewksbury investigation" report. Energetic action by the trustees and other State officials commanded the immediate attention of his Excellency Governor Butler and the legislature, and so favorably impressed them with the needs of rebuilding that a moderate appropriation was made and the work at once begun. Lack of space forbids recording minutely the detail of development and reorganization of the past sixteen years and of the evolution also of the Asylum for Insane Criminals within the same period. The plans at the beginning contemplated little change of purpose.

The rapid burning of the great wooden edifice on a calm summer morning, and the utter helplessness of fire-fighting, as witnessed by those closely associated with the institution, deeply impressed them when they reflected what might have, and certainly would have, been the result, had this conflagration occurred during a bleak nor'-wester or driving north-easter. A fearful holocaust was almost certain. There is little wonder that they at once resolved that reasonable investment in fire-proof construction should be one fundamental in the future work. It was also further resolved that convenience and simplicity should not be sacrificed for architectural pride and decoration, and it is a pleasure to note that the trustees have religiously adhered to these principles in every enlargement since made. The development to date is not from a preconceived plan as a whole, but rather a collection of additions from time to time as demands required. The name was changed in 1887 by a substitution of the word "farm" for that of "workhouse" in deference to the presence of insane paupers. The State Farm now contains three departments: the Prison, to which any criminal court may commit males and females for misdemeanor offences; the Almshouse and Hospital, which admits State paupers from Southeastern Massachusetts; and the State Asylum for Insane Criminals.

To this asylum may be committed by the superior courts insane males charged with or convicted of crime, and by other processes insane male convicts from all the prisons of the Commonwealth. The normal capacity of the whole institution is about 1,500 inmates, and is one of the largest in the State. It contains 762 single rooms and cells and 39 open wards, containing 332,714 square feet of floor-space. The farm acreage is 716.

Bridgewater and vicinity have always been identified in the management of the institution; and among those of notably long service may be mentioned the Hon. Joshua E. Crane, a trustee for twelve years, Dr. Edward Sawyer, visiting physician twenty-six years, and Dr. Calvin Pratt, visiting and consulting physician for the past twenty-five years and still in office.

The government of supervision was vested in a board of three inspectors till 1872, since by a board of trustees of five members till 1884, and seven since, two of whom have been women; the executive government, by three superintendents to date, serving fifteen, thirteen, and sixteen years respectively. The inspectors and trustees have been represented by twenty-seven gentlemen and seven ladies, and in forty-four years over forty thousand inmates have been committed to their care.

The services of these honorable and distinguished citizens have been gratuitous, but none the less arduous and devoted on this account. Their labors have been to make the institution an influence for the improvement of our unfortunate and defective fellow-men and an agent for the protection of society.

HOLLIS M. BLACKSTONE.

MINISTRIES.

The early ministries of the First Parishes are given in the chapters on the towns.

WEST BRIDGEWATER.

First Congregational (Unitarian, or First Parish).

Richard Stone, 1834-42; Darius Forbes, 1845-47; J. G. Forman, 1844-51; R. A. Ballou, 1852-56; S. B. Flagg, 1857-58; Ira Bailey, 1857-60; D. S. M. Potter, 1860-62; W. B. Thayer, 1863-64; N. O. Chaffee, 1864-65; T. L. Dean, 1865-67; J. G. Forman, 1867-70; F. B. Hamblett, 1871-76; J. W. Fitch, 1876-77; D. H. Montgomery, 1877-80; C. C. Carpenter, 1880-83; W. Brown, 1883-88; Samuel Hamlet, 1888-94; E. B. Maglathlin, 1894.

Baptist.

Bartlett Pease, 1838-41; S. S. Laighton, 1841-42; Caleb Benson, 1842-44; P. S. Whitman, 1845-46; Jeremiah Kelley, 1846-47; Silas Hall, 1847; A. W. Carr, 1847-49; G. S. Stockwell, 1851-53; Cephas Pasco, 1859-71; Joseph Barber, 1871-76; H. H. Beaman, 1876-81; J. W. Dick, 1881-82; W. S. Walker, 1883-85; G. B. Lawton, 1889-94; E. M. Bartlett, 1894-97; W. L. Smith, 1897.

Methodist Episcopal.

E. J. P. Colger, 1841-42; S. W. Coggeshall, 1843; P. Townsend, 1844-45; A. M. Swinerton, 1846-47; D. Webb, 1848-49; T. Hardman, 1850; F. Gavitt, 1851-52; J. M. Worcester, 1853-54; E. B. Hinckley, 1855-56; S. Benson, 1857-59; H. D. Robinson, 1860; C. Hammond, 1861; J. C. Allen, 1862-63; F. Sears, 1864-65; W. Eld, 1866-67; J. Mathews, 1868; P. Cronden, 1869; P. Townsend, 1870-71; E. G. Babcock, 1872; B. Sayer, 1873-74; E. A. Boyden, 1875; J. W. Sutherland, 1876; A. McCord, 1877; G. E. Luther, 1878; D. M. Rogers, 1879-80; T. B. Gurney, 1881-82; J. A. Rood, 1883-85; G. E. Dunbar, 1886-87; R. F. Kellogg, 1888-90; R. Clark, 1891-93; E. S. Hammond, 1894-95; W. B. Heath, 1896.

EAST BRIDGEWATER.

First Parish.

S. A. Devens, 1837-38; G. A. Williams, 1840-41; I. H. Blanchard, 1842; N. Whitman, 1844-52; J. H. Phipps, 1853-61; S. Farrington, 1861-64; F. C. Williams, 1865-70; John W. Quimby, 1871.

Union Church (Congregational).

Baalis Sanford, 1827-49; P. Wilcox, 1851-60; H. D. Woodworth, 1860-62; N. D. Broughton, 1862-66; J. K. Aldrich, 1868-70; A. Dodge, 1870-74; D. W. Richardson, 1874-79; P. M. Griffin, 1880-90; M. S. Kautman, 1891-93; F. H. Palmer, 1893-98; Granville Yager, 1898.

New Jerusalem Church (in Elmwood).

A. Howard, 1830-38; J. Scott, 1843-46; T. B. Hayward, 1846-49; J. P. Perry, 1850-53; E. Smith, 1853-56; T. O. Paine, 1856-95; Clarence Lathbury, 1895.

Methodist Episcopal.

Carlos Banning, 1857-58; C. H. Payne, 1859-60; W. H. Stetson, 1861-62; J. W. Willet, 1863; W. F. Farrington, 1864-66; J. F. Sheffield, 1867-68; H. H. Martin, 1869-70; S. A. Winsor, 1871-72; G. W. Anderson, 1872-74; G. W. Ballou, 1875-77; W. F. Smith, 1878-80; F. A. Crafts, 1881-82; E. S. Fletcher, 1883-85; R. Burn, 1886-88; J. N. Geisler, 1889-91; L. H. Massey, 1892; M. B. Wilson, 1893-96; N. B. Cook, 1897.

St. John (Catholic).

In charge of the resident pastor of the Bridgewater church.

BRIDGEWATER.

First Parish (or First Congregational Society), Unitarian.

T. P. Doggett, 1833-44; Claudius Bradford, 1845-51; J. J. Putnam, 1856-64; G. Dexter, 1865-66; G. H. Hosmer, 1868-78; A. E. Goodnough, 1879-81; J. A. Wilson, 1882-83; S. B. Flagg, 1885; T. W. Brown, 1886-92; Charles A. Allen, 1893.

Central Square Congregational.

Ebenezer Gay, 1823-41; S. S. Tappan, 1842-44; D. Brigham, 1845-58; J. M. Prince, 1859; Ebenezer Douglas, 1862-67; H. D. Walker, 1868-79; J. C. Bodwell, 1880-86; W. W. Fay, 1886-88; Elbert S. Porter, 1889.

Trinity (Protestant Episcopal).

Mathias Monroe, 1831-35; H. Blackeller, 1838-43; N. E. Marble, 1844-45; Asa Eaton, D.D., 1850-58; A. L. Baury, 1858-66; C. C. Harris, 1866-68; W. Warland, 1868-70; B. R. Gifford, 1871-75; W. H. Fultz, J. Greathead, and J. Jenks, successively, 1875-82; J. M. Peck, 1883-85; L. L. Ward, 1885-87; J. J. Cressey, 1887-93; F. Edwards, 1893-96; S. S. Marquis, 1896-99; G. F. Smythe, 1899.

New Jerusalem Church (Swedenborgian).

Eleazer Smith, 1824-26; Samuel Worcester, 1833-39; Th. Rodman, 1844-63; T. B. Hayward, 1864-68; T. F. Wright, Ph.D., 1869-89; Louis Rich, 1889-90; G. S. Wheeler, 1890.

Scotland Trinitarian Congregational.

Stetson Raymond, 1836-51; Joshua Huntington, 1851; D. D. Tappan, 1851-52; Cyrus Mann, 1852-53; J. D. Farnsworth, 1853-54; Otis Rockwood, 1855-56; J. C. Seagraves, 1857-65; H. P. Leonard, 1865-67; A. G. Duncan, 1867-73; I. Dunham, 1873-77; C. W. Wood, 1878-88; J. C. White, 1888-94; E. L. Hunt, 1894-95; E. S. Porter, 1895-96; Ira A. Smith, 1896.

St. Thomas Aquinas (Catholic).

Lawrence S. McMahon, afterward bishop of the diocese of Hartford, 1863-64; Bernard O'Reilly, 1864-66; M. J. Maguire, 1867-69; John A. Conlin, 1869-88; William Ed. Kelley, 1888.

Methodist Episcopal.

G. H. Baker, 1874; J. R. Ward, W. G. Wilson, 1875; T. J. Everett, 1876-77; C. H. Morgan, 1878; G. W. Coon, 1879; W. F. Farrington, 1879-80; J. B. Hengeley, 1881-82; W. A. Wright, 1883; E. S. Fletcher, 1884-85; J. A. Rand, 1886; G. E. Dunbar, 1887; R. J. Kellogg, 1888; J. N. Geisler, 1889; G. Bernreuter, 1892; R. E. Smith, 1891; L. E. Lovejoy, 1892-94; J. F. Porter, 1895; R. C. Grove, 1896-98; W. F. Taylor, 1899.

First Baptist.

Wesley L. Smith, 1897, who has also been pastor of the Baptist church in West Bridgewater since 1897.

THE OLD BRIDGEWATER HISTORICAL SOCIETY.

THE object of this society is the "collection, preservation, and publication of material which shall contribute to the history of the colonial township of Bridgewater." It was organized April 19, 1894. Its officers are: President, Hon. B. W. Harris, of East Bridgewater; Vice-Presidents, James S. Allen (successor to the late William Allen of East Bridgewater), F. E. Howard of West Bridgewater, G. M. Hooper of Bridgewater, and L. W. Puffer of Brockton; corresponding secretary and librarian, J. E. Crane, of Bridgewater; recording secretary, F. E. Sweet, of Bridgewater; treasurer, Anna W. Bates, of Bridgewater (succeeding F. F. Murdock and I. N. Nutter). A considerable sum has been pledged toward the erection of a fire-proof building on land generously offered in West Bridgewater by Vice-President F. E. Howard, where may be safely kept the society's valuable books, manuscripts, and relics. Donations of articles of historic value, as well as contributions to the building fund, are solicited from all who are interested.

C. F. DAHLBERG,

973 South Main Street,
CAMPELLO.

Headquarters for Plumbing and Heating. Agent for Magee and Smith-Anthony Furnaces and Ranges.

WILLIAMS & MAYO,

Provision Dealers,

Broad Street, Bridgewater, Mass.

USE COLE'S No. 10.
THE GREAT COLD-KILLER.

Price, 25 cents and $1.00.

PREPARED ONLY BY

O. B. COLE, Pharmacist,
BRIDGEWATER, MASS.

Ranges, Heating Stoves, Coal-hods, Shovels, Pokers, Sieves, Hardware, Tinware, Agateware.

Furnaces set and repaired.

J. B. ROGERS,

BRIDGEWATER.

SOUVENIR SPOONS

engraved to order from

PHOTOGRAPHS.

H. A. CLARK, Jeweller,

CENTRAL SQUARE, - - - - BRIDGEWATER.

GEORGE A. CONGDON,

MAKER OF ....
MEN'S CLOTHES,

No. 1 Broadway, Room 9,
TAUNTON, MASS.

FINE MILLINERY.

I have now on show all the latest models of Hats and Bonnets for fall and winter wear, and invite the ladies of Bridgewater to call and inspect the same.

A. F. WASTCOAT, 57 Main St.,
TAUNTON.

Take WILCOX'S
Beef, Wine, and Iron

For an Appetizer and Tonic.

Good all the year round, like the "Bridgewater Book."

WILCOX'S DRUG STORE, - BRIDGEWATER.
Leading Periodicals for sale.

FRANK N. CHURCHILL,

DEALER IN
DRY AND
FANCY GOODS,

GENTLEMEN'S FURNISHINGS, HATS AND CAPS,

CENTRAL SQUARE,
BRIDGEWATER.

D. B. MONROE, ∴ ∴

BOOTS, SHOES, RUBBERS,
Trunks, Bags, and Umbrellas.
Also the GOLD SEAL RUBBERS,
the best in the world.

BANK BUILDING, CENTRE ST.,
MIDDLEBORO, MASS.

MRS. G. A. PERKINS,

MILLINERY.

ORDER WORK A SPECIALTY.

Mourning Goods
promptly furnished at reasonable prices.

MAIN STREET, MIDDLEBORO.

Opposite Soule's Furniture Store.

FINE MILLINERY.

M. A. WENTWORTH & COMPANY,
No. 61 CENTRE STREET,
MIDDLEBORO, MASS.

PASZTOR & KLAR,

BAKERS.

ICE-CREAM PARLORS.

59 CENTRE STREET, MIDDLEBORO.

CHARLES A. CLARK & CO.,

DRY GOODS,
CLOAKS, AND
SUITS.

51 and 53 CENTRE ST., MIDDLEBORO,
MASS.

CRYSTAL CREAMERY CO.,

20 CENTRE STREET, BROCKTON,

TELEPHONE 262-3,

AND 55 CITY SQUARE, TAUNTON,

Where you can always get GOOD
BUTTER.

CREASY has a
fine line of trimmed hats.
$3 each.

CREASY has
ladies' bonnets. $3 each.
22 Centre Street,
Brockton.

SMITH & HATHAWAY,

PHARMACISTS,

MIDDLEBORO, - - - MASS.

Prescription compounding our specialty.
Orders by mail promptly filled.

ESTABLISHED 1820.

MILLAR & WELTCH,

Prescription
Opticians ...

And Dealers in Optical Goods.

ALSO

Cameras and
Supplies ....

38 WEST STREET, - BOSTON.

WHITMAN, SPARROW & CO.,

DRY GOODS.

Centre Street, Middleboro, Mass.

A. I. SIMMONS,

DEALER IN

MEAT AND PROVISIONS.

BRIDGEWATER.

House Heating, Hot Water, Steam, and Hot Air

PLUMBING.

AGENT FOR

GLENWOOD LINE

OF

RANGES AND HEATERS.

Fairbanks' Hardware Store,
Bridgewater.

Established 1863.

Our Store is a

BARGAIN CENTRE

and the birthplace of

LOW PRICES.

Middleboro Clothing Company,

16 Centre Street,
Middleboro, Mass.

Come and see what a look may save you.

CARPENTER & TREMAINE,

Electrical Contractors

AND DEALERS IN ALL KINDS OF

Electrical Supplies.

Electrical construction work and repairs done in best possible manner.

Telephone   CARPENTER & TREMAINE,
37 Belmont Street, Brockton.

Important Information!

COLBY'S CLOTHING STORE is one of the largest Clothing Stores in Massachusetts. The assortment of

SUITS, OVERCOATS, HORSE CLOTHING, TRUNKS, HATS and RUBBER CLOTHING

is enormous. It will pay you to visit this establishment.

Colby's Clothing House,
21 to 23 Main Street, Taunton.

Christmas will soon be with us.

We have bought in anticipation of a large sale, and can show a complete line of Children's Rockers, Rocking Horses, and Doll Carriages.

Howard, Clark & Co.,
85 Main Street, Brockton.

MORTON BROTHERS.

LAUNDRY.

R. J. CASEY, Agent,

BRIDGEWATER, MASSACHUSETTS.

CHARLES H. WASHBURN,

FURNITURE,

Crockery, and House-furnishing Goods.

No. 12 UNION BLOCK,

TAUNTON.

FOR THE HOLIDAYS.

Large stock of Pocket and Table Cutlery, Skates, Sleds, etc., at : :

F. R. WASHBURN'S

HARDWARE STORE,
15 Union Block, Taunton.

A. J. BARKER,

DRUGGIST, APOTHECARY,
AND STATIONER :: :: :: ::

10 UNION BLOCK,

TAUNTON, MASS.

C. R. DICKERMAN,

DENTIST.

GOLD AND BRIDGE WORK A SPECIALTY.

46 CITY SQUARE,

TAUNTON.

FRANK H. BOWERS,

52 Main Street, Taunton.

DIAMONDS,
WATCHES,
JEWELRY,
SILVERWARE, AND
NOVELTIES.

Everything up-to-date.   FINE WATCH REPAIRING.

WE solicit a share of your trade. Give us a call and you will see one of the largest lines of CLOTHING and GENTLEMEN'S FURNISHINGS in Bristol County.

STANDARD CLOTHING CO.,

52 AND 54 CITY SQUARE, TAUNTON.

ELIAS MILLBANK,

FUNERAL DIRECTOR

AND

EMBALMER.

14 UNION BLOCK,
TAUNTON, MASS.

H. A. CHURCHILL & CO.

HAVE THE LARGEST LINE OF

BICYCLES.

REPAIRING GUARANTEED.
CASH OR INSTALMENTS.   PARTS.
    SUNDRIES.

31 EAST ELM STREET, BROCKTON.

TAUNTON PUBLIC MARKET.

WHOLESALE AND

RETAIL MARKET.

12 MAIN STREET.

TELEPHONE CONNECTION.

KENNEDY BROTHERS,

FURNITURE AND PIANO MOVING.

Agents for MAGEE RANGES and HEATERS. Tin, Sheet Iron and Copper Work. Stove and Furnace repairs of all kinds at lowest prices. Largest house of its kind in city. When in doubt, give us a call. Stoves stored at reasonable prices.

OFFICE AND STORE, 36 SCHOOL STREET, BROCKTON, MASS.

M. J. BRENNAN, Manager.   Open evenings till ten o'clock.

F. E. FULLER & CO.,

DEALERS IN

DRY AND FANCY GOODS,

LADIES' AND GENTLEMEN'S FURNISHING GOODS, CARPETS, AND CURTAINS, BOOTS, SHOES AND RUBBERS.

PAPER HANGINGS, TOILET SOAPS, STATIONERY, ETC.

CENTRAL STREET,
EAST BRIDGEWATER, MASS.

L. A. FLAGG,

DEALER IN

GROCERIES, STATIONERY, SMALL WARES, AND HARDWARE.

Paints, Oils, Varnishes, and Window Glass, also Grass and Garden Seed.

ELMWOOD, MASS.

HERMAN S. HEWETT & CO.,

JEWELLERS AND OPTICIANS,

119 MAIN STREET,
BROCKTON.

F. S. FAXON, D.D.S.

CAREFUL AND SCIENTIFIC TREATMENT OF THE NATURAL TEETH.

183 MAIN STREET, BROCKTON.

FRANK SMITH,

APOTHECARY,

EAST BRIDGEWATER, MASS.

E. L. COOK,

MANUFACTURER OF

BUILDING, SEWER, PAVING & EXTRA PALLET

BRICK.

MEMBER OF MASTER BUILDERS' EXCHANGE, 166 DEVONSHIRE STREET, BOSTON.

Office and Works: Five minutes' walk south of Titicut Station.   Post-office: STATE FARM, MASS.

NEW BEDFORD

The wealthy old whaling city, the richest in America, size considered, demands that its merchants supply fine goods.

NEW BEDFORD, the busy manufacturing centre, demands that its merchants supply merchandise within the purchasing power of its industrial people.

Both these requirements

are generously met in our great house-furnishing establishment. We operate the largest store in this section of the State.

We carry an enormous stock.

We sell at absolutely the lowest prices.

Carpets,
Furniture,
Bedding,
Window
Shades,
Draperies,
Wall Papers,
Crockery,
Kitchen
Supplies,
and
Ranges.

We right all matters that go wrong between our salespeople and our customers.

We cheerfully pay money back for any merchandise returned, for any cause or dissatisfaction whatever.

We want to do business with you.

A postal from you will bring a prompt reply to any inquiries you choose to make.

You cannot know how cheaply we sell until you write us a letter, or, better still, make us a visit.

Charles F. Wing, 34-38 Purchase St.,
NEW BEDFORD, MASS.

L. F. WILLIAMS,

PRINTER AND PUBLISHER,

Independent Block, Central Square, BRIDGEWATER. . .

Estimates given on Printing of every character. All work delivered promptly. Publisher of Bridgewater *Independent.* Price $2.00 per year.

H. S. HUTCHINSON & CO.,

Booksellers & Stationers,

NEW BEDFORD, MASS.

Largest Book-store in South-eastern Massachusetts.

PEARCE'S CAFE

For Ladies and Gentlemen.

257 UNION STREET,
NEW BEDFORD, MASS.

A. PRATT'S

FIRST-CLASS

Model Cafe and Restaurant.

American and European Plan.
Meals at all Hours.

40 Main Street, TAUNTON, MASS.

M. W. Tillinghast,

Ladies' and Gentlemen's

RESTAURANT.

85 and 110 Westminster Street,
PROVIDENCE, R.I.

G. A. Thatcher, D.D.S.

DENTAL OFFICE,

63 MAIN STREET, BROCKTON.

LADIES!

The Latest and Most Correct Styles in

MILLINERY

can always be found at
MRS. LENA WADE-WHITMAN'S,
27 Centre Street, BROCKTON.

MOURNING WORK A SPECIALTY.

E. D. FRASIER,

Hair Dressing and Bathing Rooms.

Bath-room open every day and Sunday forenoon.

8 CENTRE STREET, BROCKTON.

HEAT YOUR HOUSE WITH A

5 Rooms,	$75
7 Rooms,	95
9 Rooms,	110
PIPING, REGISTERS, ETC., ALL COMPLETE.	

DIGHTON FURNACE.

If your old furnace has given out, see what it will cost to repair it, then write to us for a price on a new DIGHTON. *Every Part Warranted.* DIGHTON FURNACE CO., Write for Catalogue. Taunton, Mass.

ESTABLISHED 1826. INCORPORATED 1866.

Presbrey Stove Lining Co.,

TAUNTON, MASS.

Fire Brick and Stove Linings.

Any Shape or Size of Fire Brick made to order from Pattern.

FIRE CLAY, GRANITE CLAY, KAOLIN, FIRE SAND, ETC., BY THE TON OR CARGO. B. C. PEIRCE, Treasurer.

William E. Beale,

Cameras and
Photographic Supplies

At Cut Prices.

84 Main Street, Brockton.

Lafayette Keith, President.
Samuel P. Gates, Treasurer.

Bridgewater Savings Bank.

Interest commences
January 1, April 1, July 1, October 1.

Dividends are declared
April and October.

The Bridgewater Inn.

A respectable and comfortable hotel with moderate prices.

George J. Alcott, Proprietor.

MESSRS.

WM. S. ANDREWS & SON

Invite you and friends to examine their stock of

"Sorosis" Shoes

For which they have secured the exclusive sale for

Middleboro, Mass.,

22 Centre St., next door to Post-office.

Daintily shod are those who wear "SOROSIS."
Any one buying a pair of shoes will have return fare paid.

WILLIAM S. PROPHETT,

DEALER IN

Established 1860.

Household Furniture of all kinds,

UNDERTAKER.   BRIDGEWATER.

Low prices.
Reliable merchandise.
Money back for the asking.

SPARE'S. THE BIG STORE.
41 Purchase Street, New Bedford, Mass.

Buy $10 worth, and we pay fare here and return.

THE LARGEST STOCK IN THIS SECTION. Garments, Dress Skirts, Wrappers, Petticoats, Silk Waists, Dress Goods, and Silks. Confectionery. Notions, Underwear. Complete Kitchen Furnishings Department.

13 departments crowded with new merchandise.   Ask the conductor to let you off at Spare's.

www.ingramcontent.com/pod-product-compliance
Lightning Source LLC
Chambersburg PA
CBHW020252090426
42735CB00010B/1892